I0816611

THIS JOURNAL BELONGS TO:

____

HEALING

Whether you're healing from the loss of a loved one, an injury, an emotional loss, or any other traumatic event, the healing process is daunting. It's natural to feel overwhelmed by change, emotion, and fear.

The most challenging step to healing is recognizing that something life-altering has happened to you. Your healing journey is a process of acknowledging, accepting, and processing the painful experience and emotions, and knowing that you will come out the other side a different, yet stronger person.

ALTHOUGH THE HEALING PROCESS and timeline are never the same for everyone, there are a few steps you can take to help you navigate your healing journey:

- **RELINQUISH YOUR EXPECTATIONS:** Understand that healing can be a difficult and painful process. Release your expectations of how it should look and how long it should take, and allow yourself to move through the process at your own pace.

- **FEEL YOUR EMOTIONS FULLY:** Don't push any distressing emotions away. Allow yourself to feel them and then feel them pass.

- **ESTABLISH NORMALCY:** Find moments of peace and comfort in your daily life through routines and the little things that you can depend on. Form habits that rejuvenate your mind and body.

- **TAKE ONE STEP AT A TIME:** Don't overwhelm yourself by trying to fix or do everything at once. Divide big tasks into little ones and understand your limits.

- **PRACTICE MINDFULNESS:** Don't let your mind retreat into the past too much or catastrophize about the future. Remember that in this present moment, everything is fine.

- **LEAN ON OTHERS:** Know that you are not alone. Surround yourself with those who love and support you, and lean on them when you need to.

- **EMBRACE JOY:** Accept that it's okay to feel joy and warmth in the wake of a traumatic event.

This journal will gently guide you through your healing journey. Learn to treat yourself with compassion, tap into your inner strength to carry you through whatever it is you have experienced, and find the peace you deserve.

MORNING REFLECTION

DATE ___/___/___

HOURS SLEPT: ______

MY MOOD THIS MORNING

POOR 1 2 3 4 5 6 7 8 9 10 GREAT

THOUGHTS I WOKE UP WITH / I WOKE UP FEELING:

THE FEELINGS I'M EXPERIENCING MOST RIGHT NOW:

GOALS FOR TODAY:

THINGS THAT CAN WAIT:

HOW I INTEND TO REJUVENATE MY MIND AND BODY TODAY:

- ☐ EXERCISING
- ☐ LISTENING TO MUSIC
- ☐ MEDITATING
- ☐ JOURNALING
- ☐ READING
- ☐ TALKING TO SOMEONE
- ☐ TIME WITH LOVED ONES
- ☐ TIME WITH A PET
- ☐ GRATITUDE/POSITIVE SELF-TALK
- ☐ TIME OUTSIDE
- ☐ DOWNTIME
- ☐ OTHER: ______

EVENING REFLECTION

POOR | MY MOOD THIS EVENING | GREAT

1 2 3 4 5 6 7 8 9 10

DIFFICULT EMOTIONS THAT I EXPERIENCED TODAY:

MOMENTS OF HAPPINESS/JOY I EXPERIENCED TODAY:

A SELF-PRAISE OR GRATITUDE:

THIS HELPED ME THE MOST TODAY:

SOMETHING I NEED HELP WITH:

MORNING REFLECTION

DATE ___/___/___

HOURS SLEPT:	POOR	MY MOOD THIS MORNING							GREAT
________	1	2	3	4	5	6	7	8	9	10

THOUGHTS I WOKE UP WITH / I WOKE UP FEELING:

THE FEELINGS I'M EXPERIENCING MOST RIGHT NOW:

GOALS FOR TODAY:

THINGS THAT CAN WAIT:

HOW I INTEND TO REJUVENATE MY MIND AND BODY TODAY:

- ☐ EXERCISING
- ☐ LISTENING TO MUSIC
- ☐ MEDITATING
- ☐ JOURNALING
- ☐ READING
- ☐ TALKING TO SOMEONE
- ☐ TIME WITH LOVED ONES
- ☐ TIME WITH A PET
- ☐ GRATITUDE/POSITIVE SELF-TALK
- ☐ TIME OUTSIDE
- ☐ DOWNTIME
- ☐ OTHER: ________

EVENING REFLECTION

POOR MY MOOD THIS EVENING GREAT

1 2 3 4 5 6 7 8 9 10

DIFFICULT EMOTIONS THAT I EXPERIENCED TODAY:

MOMENTS OF HAPPINESS/JOY I EXPERIENCED TODAY:

A SELF-PRAISE OR GRATITUDE:

THIS HELPED ME THE MOST TODAY:

SOMETHING I NEED HELP WITH:

MORNING REFLECTION

DATE ___/___/___

HOURS SLEPT: __________

MY MOOD THIS MORNING

POOR 1 2 3 4 5 6 7 8 9 10 GREAT

THOUGHTS I WOKE UP WITH / I WOKE UP FEELING:

THE FEELINGS I'M EXPERIENCING MOST RIGHT NOW:

GOALS FOR TODAY:

THINGS THAT CAN WAIT:

HOW I INTEND TO REJUVENATE MY MIND AND BODY TODAY:

- ☐ EXERCISING
- ☐ LISTENING TO MUSIC
- ☐ MEDITATING
- ☐ JOURNALING
- ☐ READING
- ☐ TALKING TO SOMEONE
- ☐ TIME WITH LOVED ONES
- ☐ TIME WITH A PET
- ☐ GRATITUDE/POSITIVE SELF-TALK
- ☐ TIME OUTSIDE
- ☐ DOWNTIME
- ☐ OTHER: __________

EVENING REFLECTION

POOR | MY MOOD THIS EVENING | GREAT

1 2 3 4 5 6 7 8 9 10

DIFFICULT EMOTIONS THAT I EXPERIENCED TODAY:

MOMENTS OF HAPPINESS/JOY I EXPERIENCED TODAY:

A SELF-PRAISE OR GRATITUDE:

THIS HELPED ME THE MOST TODAY:

SOMETHING I NEED HELP WITH:

MORNING REFLECTION

DATE ___/___/___

HOURS SLEPT:	POOR	MY MOOD THIS MORNING							GREAT
________	1	2	3	4	5	6	7	8	9	10

THOUGHTS I WOKE UP WITH / I WOKE UP FEELING:

THE FEELINGS I'M EXPERIENCING MOST RIGHT NOW:

GOALS FOR TODAY:

THINGS THAT CAN WAIT:

HOW I INTEND TO REJUVENATE MY MIND AND BODY TODAY:

- ☐ EXERCISING
- ☐ LISTENING TO MUSIC
- ☐ MEDITATING
- ☐ JOURNALING
- ☐ READING
- ☐ TALKING TO SOMEONE
- ☐ TIME WITH LOVED ONES
- ☐ TIME WITH A PET
- ☐ GRATITUDE/POSITIVE SELF-TALK
- ☐ TIME OUTSIDE
- ☐ DOWNTIME
- ☐ OTHER: ____________

EVENING REFLECTION

POOR | MY MOOD THIS EVENING | GREAT

1 2 3 4 5 6 7 8 9 10

DIFFICULT EMOTIONS THAT I EXPERIENCED TODAY:

MOMENTS OF HAPPINESS/JOY I EXPERIENCED TODAY:

A SELF-PRAISE OR GRATITUDE:

THIS HELPED ME THE MOST TODAY:

SOMETHING I NEED HELP WITH:

MORNING REFLECTION

DATE ___/___/___

HOURS SLEPT: __________

POOR — MY MOOD THIS MORNING — GREAT

1 2 3 4 5 6 7 8 9 10

THOUGHTS I WOKE UP WITH / I WOKE UP FEELING:

THE FEELINGS I'M EXPERIENCING MOST RIGHT NOW:

GOALS FOR TODAY:

THINGS THAT CAN WAIT:

HOW I INTEND TO REJUVENATE MY MIND AND BODY TODAY:

- ☐ EXERCISING
- ☐ LISTENING TO MUSIC
- ☐ MEDITATING
- ☐ JOURNALING
- ☐ READING
- ☐ TALKING TO SOMEONE
- ☐ TIME WITH LOVED ONES
- ☐ TIME WITH A PET
- ☐ GRATITUDE/POSITIVE SELF-TALK
- ☐ TIME OUTSIDE
- ☐ DOWNTIME
- ☐ OTHER: __________

EVENING REFLECTION

POOR MY MOOD THIS EVENING GREAT

1 2 3 4 5 6 7 8 9 10

DIFFICULT EMOTIONS THAT I EXPERIENCED TODAY:

MOMENTS OF HAPPINESS/JOY I EXPERIENCED TODAY:

A SELF-PRAISE OR GRATITUDE:

THIS HELPED ME THE MOST TODAY:

SOMETHING I NEED HELP WITH:

MORNING REFLECTION

DATE ___/___/___

HOURS SLEPT: ____________

POOR — MY MOOD THIS MORNING — GREAT

1 2 3 4 5 6 7 8 9 10

THOUGHTS I WOKE UP WITH / I WOKE UP FEELING:

THE FEELINGS I'M EXPERIENCING MOST RIGHT NOW:

GOALS FOR TODAY:

THINGS THAT CAN WAIT:

HOW I INTEND TO REJUVENATE MY MIND AND BODY TODAY:

- ☐ EXERCISING
- ☐ LISTENING TO MUSIC
- ☐ MEDITATING
- ☐ JOURNALING
- ☐ READING
- ☐ TALKING TO SOMEONE
- ☐ TIME WITH LOVED ONES
- ☐ TIME WITH A PET
- ☐ GRATITUDE/POSITIVE SELF-TALK
- ☐ TIME OUTSIDE
- ☐ DOWNTIME
- ☐ OTHER: ____________

EVENING REFLECTION

POOR MY MOOD THIS EVENING GREAT

1 2 3 4 5 6 7 8 9 10

DIFFICULT EMOTIONS THAT I EXPERIENCED TODAY:

MOMENTS OF HAPPINESS/JOY I EXPERIENCED TODAY:

A SELF-PRAISE OR GRATITUDE:

THIS HELPED ME THE MOST TODAY:

SOMETHING I NEED HELP WITH:

MORNING REFLECTION

DATE ___/___/___

HOURS SLEPT: ______________

POOR — MY MOOD THIS MORNING — GREAT

1 2 3 4 5 6 7 8 9 10

THOUGHTS I WOKE UP WITH / I WOKE UP FEELING:

THE FEELINGS I'M EXPERIENCING MOST RIGHT NOW:

GOALS FOR TODAY:

THINGS THAT CAN WAIT:

HOW I INTEND TO REJUVENATE MY MIND AND BODY TODAY:

- ☐ EXERCISING
- ☐ LISTENING TO MUSIC
- ☐ MEDITATING
- ☐ JOURNALING
- ☐ READING
- ☐ TALKING TO SOMEONE
- ☐ TIME WITH LOVED ONES
- ☐ TIME WITH A PET
- ☐ GRATITUDE/POSITIVE SELF-TALK
- ☐ TIME OUTSIDE
- ☐ DOWNTIME
- ☐ OTHER: ______________

EVENING REFLECTION

POOR | MY MOOD THIS EVENING | GREAT

1 2 3 4 5 6 7 8 9 10

DIFFICULT EMOTIONS THAT I EXPERIENCED TODAY:

MOMENTS OF HAPPINESS/JOY I EXPERIENCED TODAY:

A SELF-PRAISE OR GRATITUDE:

THIS HELPED ME THE MOST TODAY:

SOMETHING I NEED HELP WITH:

MORNING REFLECTION

DATE ___/___/___

HOURS SLEPT: ____________

POOR			MY MOOD THIS MORNING						GREAT
1	2	3	4	5	6	7	8	9	10

THOUGHTS I WOKE UP WITH / I WOKE UP FEELING:

THE FEELINGS I'M EXPERIENCING MOST RIGHT NOW:

GOALS FOR TODAY:

THINGS THAT CAN WAIT:

HOW I INTEND TO REJUVENATE MY MIND AND BODY TODAY:

- ☐ EXERCISING
- ☐ LISTENING TO MUSIC
- ☐ MEDITATING
- ☐ JOURNALING
- ☐ READING
- ☐ TALKING TO SOMEONE
- ☐ TIME WITH LOVED ONES
- ☐ TIME WITH A PET
- ☐ GRATITUDE/POSITIVE SELF-TALK
- ☐ TIME OUTSIDE
- ☐ DOWNTIME
- ☐ OTHER: ____________

EVENING REFLECTION

POOR MY MOOD THIS EVENING GREAT

1 2 3 4 5 6 7 8 9 10

DIFFICULT EMOTIONS THAT I EXPERIENCED TODAY:

MOMENTS OF HAPPINESS/JOY I EXPERIENCED TODAY:

A SELF-PRAISE OR GRATITUDE:

THIS HELPED ME THE MOST TODAY:

SOMETHING I NEED HELP WITH:

MORNING REFLECTION

DATE ___/___/___

HOURS SLEPT: ____________

POOR MY MOOD THIS MORNING GREAT

1 2 3 4 5 6 7 8 9 10

THOUGHTS I WOKE UP WITH / I WOKE UP FEELING:

THE FEELINGS I'M EXPERIENCING MOST RIGHT NOW:

GOALS FOR TODAY:

THINGS THAT CAN WAIT:

HOW I INTEND TO REJUVENATE MY MIND AND BODY TODAY:

- ☐ EXERCISING
- ☐ LISTENING TO MUSIC
- ☐ MEDITATING
- ☐ JOURNALING
- ☐ READING
- ☐ TALKING TO SOMEONE
- ☐ TIME WITH LOVED ONES
- ☐ TIME WITH A PET
- ☐ GRATITUDE/POSITIVE SELF-TALK
- ☐ TIME OUTSIDE
- ☐ DOWNTIME
- ☐ OTHER: ____________

EVENING REFLECTION

POOR — MY MOOD THIS EVENING — GREAT

1 2 3 4 5 6 7 8 9 10

DIFFICULT EMOTIONS THAT I EXPERIENCED TODAY:

MOMENTS OF HAPPINESS/JOY I EXPERIENCED TODAY:

A SELF-PRAISE OR GRATITUDE:

THIS HELPED ME THE MOST TODAY:

SOMETHING I NEED HELP WITH:

MORNING REFLECTION

DATE ___/___/___

HOURS SLEPT: ____________

POOR		MY MOOD THIS MORNING							GREAT
1	2	3	4	5	6	7	8	9	10

THOUGHTS I WOKE UP WITH / I WOKE UP FEELING:

THE FEELINGS I'M EXPERIENCING MOST RIGHT NOW:

GOALS FOR TODAY:

THINGS THAT CAN WAIT:

HOW I INTEND TO REJUVENATE MY MIND AND BODY TODAY:

- ☐ EXERCISING
- ☐ LISTENING TO MUSIC
- ☐ MEDITATING
- ☐ JOURNALING
- ☐ READING
- ☐ TALKING TO SOMEONE
- ☐ TIME WITH LOVED ONES
- ☐ TIME WITH A PET
- ☐ GRATITUDE/POSITIVE SELF-TALK
- ☐ TIME OUTSIDE
- ☐ DOWNTIME
- ☐ OTHER: ____________

EVENING REFLECTION

POOR MY MOOD THIS EVENING GREAT

1 2 3 4 5 6 7 8 9 10

DIFFICULT EMOTIONS THAT I EXPERIENCED TODAY:

MOMENTS OF HAPPINESS/JOY I EXPERIENCED TODAY:

A SELF-PRAISE OR GRATITUDE:

THIS HELPED ME THE MOST TODAY:

SOMETHING I NEED HELP WITH:

MORNING REFLECTION

DATE ___/___/___

HOURS SLEPT: ______________

POOR — MY MOOD THIS MORNING — GREAT

1 2 3 4 5 6 7 8 9 10

THOUGHTS I WOKE UP WITH / I WOKE UP FEELING:

THE FEELINGS I'M EXPERIENCING MOST RIGHT NOW:

GOALS FOR TODAY:

THINGS THAT CAN WAIT:

HOW I INTEND TO REJUVENATE MY MIND AND BODY TODAY:

- ☐ EXERCISING
- ☐ LISTENING TO MUSIC
- ☐ MEDITATING
- ☐ JOURNALING
- ☐ READING
- ☐ TALKING TO SOMEONE
- ☐ TIME WITH LOVED ONES
- ☐ TIME WITH A PET
- ☐ GRATITUDE/POSITIVE SELF-TALK
- ☐ TIME OUTSIDE
- ☐ DOWNTIME
- ☐ OTHER: ______________

EVENING REFLECTION

POOR MY MOOD THIS EVENING GREAT

1 2 3 4 5 6 7 8 9 10

DIFFICULT EMOTIONS THAT I EXPERIENCED TODAY:

MOMENTS OF HAPPINESS/JOY I EXPERIENCED TODAY:

A SELF-PRAISE OR GRATITUDE:

THIS HELPED ME THE MOST TODAY:

SOMETHING I NEED HELP WITH:

MORNING REFLECTION

DATE ___/___/___

HOURS SLEPT: ________

MY MOOD THIS MORNING

POOR 1 2 3 4 5 6 7 8 9 10 GREAT

THOUGHTS I WOKE UP WITH / I WOKE UP FEELING:

THE FEELINGS I'M EXPERIENCING MOST RIGHT NOW:

GOALS FOR TODAY:

THINGS THAT CAN WAIT:

HOW I INTEND TO REJUVENATE MY MIND AND BODY TODAY:

- ☐ EXERCISING
- ☐ LISTENING TO MUSIC
- ☐ MEDITATING
- ☐ JOURNALING
- ☐ READING
- ☐ TALKING TO SOMEONE
- ☐ TIME WITH LOVED ONES
- ☐ TIME WITH A PET
- ☐ GRATITUDE/POSITIVE SELF-TALK
- ☐ TIME OUTSIDE
- ☐ DOWNTIME
- ☐ OTHER: ________

EVENING REFLECTION

POOR MY MOOD THIS EVENING GREAT

1 2 3 4 5 6 7 8 9 10

DIFFICULT EMOTIONS THAT I EXPERIENCED TODAY:

MOMENTS OF HAPPINESS/JOY I EXPERIENCED TODAY:

A SELF-PRAISE OR GRATITUDE:

THIS HELPED ME THE MOST TODAY:

SOMETHING I NEED HELP WITH:

MORNING REFLECTION

DATE ___/___/___

HOURS SLEPT: ______________

MY MOOD THIS MORNING

POOR 1 2 3 4 5 6 7 8 9 10 GREAT

THOUGHTS I WOKE UP WITH / I WOKE UP FEELING:

THE FEELINGS I'M EXPERIENCING MOST RIGHT NOW:

GOALS FOR TODAY:

THINGS THAT CAN WAIT:

HOW I INTEND TO REJUVENATE MY MIND AND BODY TODAY:

- ☐ EXERCISING
- ☐ LISTENING TO MUSIC
- ☐ MEDITATING
- ☐ JOURNALING
- ☐ READING
- ☐ TALKING TO SOMEONE
- ☐ TIME WITH LOVED ONES
- ☐ TIME WITH A PET
- ☐ GRATITUDE/POSITIVE SELF-TALK
- ☐ TIME OUTSIDE
- ☐ DOWNTIME
- ☐ OTHER: ______________

EVENING REFLECTION

POOR MY MOOD THIS EVENING GREAT

1 2 3 4 5 6 7 8 9 10

DIFFICULT EMOTIONS THAT I EXPERIENCED TODAY:

MOMENTS OF HAPPINESS/JOY I EXPERIENCED TODAY:

A SELF-PRAISE OR GRATITUDE:

THIS HELPED ME THE MOST TODAY:

SOMETHING I NEED HELP WITH:

MORNING REFLECTION

DATE ___/___/___

HOURS SLEPT: ____________

POOR			MY MOOD THIS MORNING						GREAT
1	2	3	4	5	6	7	8	9	10

THOUGHTS I WOKE UP WITH / I WOKE UP FEELING:

THE FEELINGS I'M EXPERIENCING MOST RIGHT NOW:

GOALS FOR TODAY:

THINGS THAT CAN WAIT:

HOW I INTEND TO REJUVENATE MY MIND AND BODY TODAY:

- ☐ EXERCISING
- ☐ LISTENING TO MUSIC
- ☐ MEDITATING
- ☐ JOURNALING
- ☐ READING
- ☐ TALKING TO SOMEONE
- ☐ TIME WITH LOVED ONES
- ☐ TIME WITH A PET
- ☐ GRATITUDE/POSITIVE SELF-TALK
- ☐ TIME OUTSIDE
- ☐ DOWNTIME
- ☐ OTHER: ____________

EVENING REFLECTION

POOR MY MOOD THIS EVENING GREAT

1 2 3 4 5 6 7 8 9 10

DIFFICULT EMOTIONS THAT I EXPERIENCED TODAY:

MOMENTS OF HAPPINESS/JOY I EXPERIENCED TODAY:

A SELF-PRAISE OR GRATITUDE:

THIS HELPED ME THE MOST TODAY:

SOMETHING I NEED HELP WITH:

MORNING REFLECTION

DATE ___/___/___

HOURS SLEPT: ___________

POOR			MY MOOD THIS MORNING						GREAT
1	2	3	4	5	6	7	8	9	10

THOUGHTS I WOKE UP WITH / I WOKE UP FEELING:

THE FEELINGS I'M EXPERIENCING MOST RIGHT NOW:

GOALS FOR TODAY:

THINGS THAT CAN WAIT:

HOW I INTEND TO REJUVENATE MY MIND AND BODY TODAY:

- ☐ EXERCISING
- ☐ LISTENING TO MUSIC
- ☐ MEDITATING
- ☐ JOURNALING
- ☐ READING
- ☐ TALKING TO SOMEONE
- ☐ TIME WITH LOVED ONES
- ☐ TIME WITH A PET
- ☐ GRATITUDE/POSITIVE SELF-TALK
- ☐ TIME OUTSIDE
- ☐ DOWNTIME
- ☐ OTHER: ___________

EVENING REFLECTION

POOR | MY MOOD THIS EVENING | GREAT

1 2 3 4 5 6 7 8 9 10

DIFFICULT EMOTIONS THAT I EXPERIENCED TODAY:

MOMENTS OF HAPPINESS/JOY I EXPERIENCED TODAY:

A SELF-PRAISE OR GRATITUDE:

THIS HELPED ME THE MOST TODAY:

SOMETHING I NEED HELP WITH:

MORNING REFLECTION

DATE ___/___/___

HOURS SLEPT: ___________

POOR — MY MOOD THIS MORNING — GREAT

1 2 3 4 5 6 7 8 9 10

THOUGHTS I WOKE UP WITH / I WOKE UP FEELING:

THE FEELINGS I'M EXPERIENCING MOST RIGHT NOW:

GOALS FOR TODAY:

THINGS THAT CAN WAIT:

HOW I INTEND TO REJUVENATE MY MIND AND BODY TODAY:

- ☐ EXERCISING
- ☐ LISTENING TO MUSIC
- ☐ MEDITATING
- ☐ JOURNALING
- ☐ READING
- ☐ TALKING TO SOMEONE
- ☐ TIME WITH LOVED ONES
- ☐ TIME WITH A PET
- ☐ GRATITUDE/POSITIVE SELF-TALK
- ☐ TIME OUTSIDE
- ☐ DOWNTIME
- ☐ OTHER: ___________

EVENING REFLECTION

POOR | MY MOOD THIS EVENING | GREAT

1 2 3 4 5 6 7 8 9 10

DIFFICULT EMOTIONS THAT I EXPERIENCED TODAY:

MOMENTS OF HAPPINESS/JOY I EXPERIENCED TODAY:

A SELF-PRAISE OR GRATITUDE:

THIS HELPED ME THE MOST TODAY:

SOMETHING I NEED HELP WITH:

MORNING REFLECTION

DATE ___/___/___

HOURS SLEPT: ____________

MY MOOD THIS MORNING

POOR 1 2 3 4 5 6 7 8 9 10 GREAT

THOUGHTS I WOKE UP WITH / I WOKE UP FEELING:

THE FEELINGS I'M EXPERIENCING MOST RIGHT NOW:

GOALS FOR TODAY:

THINGS THAT CAN WAIT:

HOW I INTEND TO REJUVENATE MY MIND AND BODY TODAY:

- ☐ EXERCISING
- ☐ LISTENING TO MUSIC
- ☐ MEDITATING
- ☐ JOURNALING
- ☐ READING
- ☐ TALKING TO SOMEONE
- ☐ TIME WITH LOVED ONES
- ☐ TIME WITH A PET
- ☐ GRATITUDE/POSITIVE SELF-TALK
- ☐ TIME OUTSIDE
- ☐ DOWNTIME
- ☐ OTHER: ____________

EVENING REFLECTION

POOR MY MOOD THIS EVENING GREAT

1 2 3 4 5 6 7 8 9 10

DIFFICULT EMOTIONS THAT I EXPERIENCED TODAY:

MOMENTS OF HAPPINESS/JOY I EXPERIENCED TODAY:

A SELF-PRAISE OR GRATITUDE:

THIS HELPED ME THE MOST TODAY:

SOMETHING I NEED HELP WITH:

MORNING REFLECTION

DATE ___/___/___

HOURS SLEPT: ____________

MY MOOD THIS MORNING

POOR 1 2 3 4 5 6 7 8 9 10 GREAT

THOUGHTS I WOKE UP WITH / I WOKE UP FEELING:

THE FEELINGS I'M EXPERIENCING MOST RIGHT NOW:

GOALS FOR TODAY:

THINGS THAT CAN WAIT:

HOW I INTEND TO REJUVENATE MY MIND AND BODY TODAY:

- ☐ EXERCISING
- ☐ LISTENING TO MUSIC
- ☐ MEDITATING
- ☐ JOURNALING
- ☐ READING
- ☐ TALKING TO SOMEONE
- ☐ TIME WITH LOVED ONES
- ☐ TIME WITH A PET
- ☐ GRATITUDE/POSITIVE SELF-TALK
- ☐ TIME OUTSIDE
- ☐ DOWNTIME
- ☐ OTHER: ____________

EVENING REFLECTION

POOR — MY MOOD THIS EVENING — GREAT

1 2 3 4 5 6 7 8 9 10

DIFFICULT EMOTIONS THAT I EXPERIENCED TODAY:

MOMENTS OF HAPPINESS/JOY I EXPERIENCED TODAY:

A SELF-PRAISE OR GRATITUDE:

THIS HELPED ME THE MOST TODAY:

SOMETHING I NEED HELP WITH:

MORNING REFLECTION

DATE ___/___/___

HOURS SLEPT: ______________

POOR — MY MOOD THIS MORNING — GREAT

1 2 3 4 5 6 7 8 9 10

THOUGHTS I WOKE UP WITH / I WOKE UP FEELING:

THE FEELINGS I'M EXPERIENCING MOST RIGHT NOW:

GOALS FOR TODAY:

THINGS THAT CAN WAIT:

HOW I INTEND TO REJUVENATE MY MIND AND BODY TODAY:

- ☐ EXERCISING
- ☐ LISTENING TO MUSIC
- ☐ MEDITATING
- ☐ JOURNALING
- ☐ READING
- ☐ TALKING TO SOMEONE
- ☐ TIME WITH LOVED ONES
- ☐ TIME WITH A PET
- ☐ GRATITUDE/POSITIVE SELF-TALK
- ☐ TIME OUTSIDE
- ☐ DOWNTIME
- ☐ OTHER: ______________

EVENING REFLECTION

POOR MY MOOD THIS EVENING GREAT

1 2 3 4 5 6 7 8 9 10

DIFFICULT EMOTIONS THAT I EXPERIENCED TODAY:

MOMENTS OF HAPPINESS/JOY I EXPERIENCED TODAY:

A SELF-PRAISE OR GRATITUDE:

THIS HELPED ME THE MOST TODAY:

SOMETHING I NEED HELP WITH:

MORNING REFLECTION

DATE ___/___/___

HOURS SLEPT: ___________

POOR — MY MOOD THIS MORNING — GREAT

1 2 3 4 5 6 7 8 9 10

THOUGHTS I WOKE UP WITH / I WOKE UP FEELING:

THE FEELINGS I'M EXPERIENCING MOST RIGHT NOW:

GOALS FOR TODAY:

THINGS THAT CAN WAIT:

HOW I INTEND TO REJUVENATE MY MIND AND BODY TODAY:

- ☐ EXERCISING
- ☐ LISTENING TO MUSIC
- ☐ MEDITATING
- ☐ JOURNALING
- ☐ READING
- ☐ TALKING TO SOMEONE
- ☐ TIME WITH LOVED ONES
- ☐ TIME WITH A PET
- ☐ GRATITUDE/POSITIVE SELF-TALK
- ☐ TIME OUTSIDE
- ☐ DOWNTIME
- ☐ OTHER: ___________

EVENING REFLECTION

POOR MY MOOD THIS EVENING GREAT

1 2 3 4 5 6 7 8 9 10

DIFFICULT EMOTIONS THAT I EXPERIENCED TODAY:

MOMENTS OF HAPPINESS/JOY I EXPERIENCED TODAY:

A SELF-PRAISE OR GRATITUDE:

THIS HELPED ME THE MOST TODAY:

SOMETHING I NEED HELP WITH:

MORNING REFLECTION

DATE ___/___/___

HOURS SLEPT: ______________

MY MOOD THIS MORNING

POOR 1 2 3 4 5 6 7 8 9 10 GREAT

THOUGHTS I WOKE UP WITH / I WOKE UP FEELING:

____
____
____
____

THE FEELINGS I'M EXPERIENCING MOST RIGHT NOW:

____
____
____
____

GOALS FOR TODAY:

____
____
____

THINGS THAT CAN WAIT:

____
____
____

HOW I INTEND TO REJUVENATE MY MIND AND BODY TODAY:

- ☐ EXERCISING
- ☐ LISTENING TO MUSIC
- ☐ MEDITATING
- ☐ JOURNALING
- ☐ READING
- ☐ TALKING TO SOMEONE
- ☐ TIME WITH LOVED ONES
- ☐ TIME WITH A PET
- ☐ GRATITUDE/POSITIVE SELF-TALK
- ☐ TIME OUTSIDE
- ☐ DOWNTIME
- ☐ OTHER: ______________

EVENING REFLECTION

POOR MY MOOD THIS EVENING GREAT

1 2 3 4 5 6 7 8 9 10

DIFFICULT EMOTIONS THAT I EXPERIENCED TODAY:

MOMENTS OF HAPPINESS/JOY I EXPERIENCED TODAY:

A SELF-PRAISE OR GRATITUDE:

THIS HELPED ME THE MOST TODAY:

SOMETHING I NEED HELP WITH:

MORNING REFLECTION

DATE ___/___/___

HOURS SLEPT: ____________

POOR			MY MOOD THIS MORNING						GREAT
1	2	3	4	5	6	7	8	9	10

THOUGHTS I WOKE UP WITH / I WOKE UP FEELING:

THE FEELINGS I'M EXPERIENCING MOST RIGHT NOW:

GOALS FOR TODAY:

THINGS THAT CAN WAIT:

HOW I INTEND TO REJUVENATE MY MIND AND BODY TODAY:

- [ ] EXERCISING
- [ ] LISTENING TO MUSIC
- [ ] MEDITATING
- [ ] JOURNALING
- [ ] READING
- [ ] TALKING TO SOMEONE
- [ ] TIME WITH LOVED ONES
- [ ] TIME WITH A PET
- [ ] GRATITUDE/POSITIVE SELF-TALK
- [ ] TIME OUTSIDE
- [ ] DOWNTIME
- [ ] OTHER: ____________

EVENING REFLECTION

POOR MY MOOD THIS EVENING GREAT

1 2 3 4 5 6 7 8 9 10

DIFFICULT EMOTIONS THAT I EXPERIENCED TODAY:

MOMENTS OF HAPPINESS/JOY I EXPERIENCED TODAY:

A SELF-PRAISE OR GRATITUDE:

THIS HELPED ME THE MOST TODAY:

SOMETHING I NEED HELP WITH:

MORNING REFLECTION

DATE ___/___/___

HOURS SLEPT: ____________

POOR			MY MOOD THIS MORNING						GREAT
1	2	3	4	5	6	7	8	9	10

THOUGHTS I WOKE UP WITH / I WOKE UP FEELING:

THE FEELINGS I'M EXPERIENCING MOST RIGHT NOW:

GOALS FOR TODAY:

THINGS THAT CAN WAIT:

HOW I INTEND TO REJUVENATE MY MIND AND BODY TODAY:

- ☐ EXERCISING
- ☐ LISTENING TO MUSIC
- ☐ MEDITATING
- ☐ JOURNALING
- ☐ READING
- ☐ TALKING TO SOMEONE
- ☐ TIME WITH LOVED ONES
- ☐ TIME WITH A PET
- ☐ GRATITUDE/POSITIVE SELF-TALK
- ☐ TIME OUTSIDE
- ☐ DOWNTIME
- ☐ OTHER: ____________

EVENING REFLECTION

POOR — MY MOOD THIS EVENING — GREAT

1 2 3 4 5 6 7 8 9 10

DIFFICULT EMOTIONS THAT I EXPERIENCED TODAY:

MOMENTS OF HAPPINESS/JOY I EXPERIENCED TODAY:

A SELF-PRAISE OR GRATITUDE:

THIS HELPED ME THE MOST TODAY:

SOMETHING I NEED HELP WITH:

MORNING REFLECTION

DATE ___/___/___

HOURS SLEPT:	POOR			MY MOOD THIS MORNING						GREAT
____________	1	2	3	4	5	6	7	8	9	10

THOUGHTS I WOKE UP WITH / I WOKE UP FEELING:

THE FEELINGS I'M EXPERIENCING MOST RIGHT NOW:

GOALS FOR TODAY:

THINGS THAT CAN WAIT:

HOW I INTEND TO REJUVENATE MY MIND AND BODY TODAY:

- ☐ EXERCISING
- ☐ LISTENING TO MUSIC
- ☐ MEDITATING
- ☐ JOURNALING
- ☐ READING
- ☐ TALKING TO SOMEONE
- ☐ TIME WITH LOVED ONES
- ☐ TIME WITH A PET
- ☐ GRATITUDE/POSITIVE SELF-TALK
- ☐ TIME OUTSIDE
- ☐ DOWNTIME
- ☐ OTHER: ____________

EVENING REFLECTION

POOR				MY MOOD THIS EVENING					GREAT
1	2	3	4	5	6	7	8	9	10

DIFFICULT EMOTIONS THAT I EXPERIENCED TODAY:

MOMENTS OF HAPPINESS/JOY I EXPERIENCED TODAY:

A SELF-PRAISE OR GRATITUDE:

THIS HELPED ME THE MOST TODAY:

SOMETHING I NEED HELP WITH:

MORNING REFLECTION

DATE ___/___/___

HOURS SLEPT: ____________

POOR — MY MOOD THIS MORNING — GREAT

1 2 3 4 5 6 7 8 9 10

THOUGHTS I WOKE UP WITH / I WOKE UP FEELING:

____

____

____

____

THE FEELINGS I'M EXPERIENCING MOST RIGHT NOW:

____

____

____

____

GOALS FOR TODAY:

____

____

____

THINGS THAT CAN WAIT:

____

____

____

HOW I INTEND TO REJUVENATE MY MIND AND BODY TODAY:

- ☐ EXERCISING
- ☐ LISTENING TO MUSIC
- ☐ MEDITATING
- ☐ JOURNALING
- ☐ READING
- ☐ TALKING TO SOMEONE
- ☐ TIME WITH LOVED ONES
- ☐ TIME WITH A PET
- ☐ GRATITUDE/POSITIVE SELF-TALK
- ☐ TIME OUTSIDE
- ☐ DOWNTIME
- ☐ OTHER: ____________

EVENING REFLECTION

POOR MY MOOD THIS EVENING GREAT

1 2 3 4 5 6 7 8 9 10

DIFFICULT EMOTIONS THAT I EXPERIENCED TODAY:

MOMENTS OF HAPPINESS/JOY I EXPERIENCED TODAY:

A SELF-PRAISE OR GRATITUDE:

THIS HELPED ME THE MOST TODAY:

SOMETHING I NEED HELP WITH:

MORNING REFLECTION

DATE ___/___/___

HOURS SLEPT:	POOR				MY MOOD THIS MORNING					GREAT
______	1	2	3	4	5	6	7	8	9	10

THOUGHTS I WOKE UP WITH / I WOKE UP FEELING:

THE FEELINGS I'M EXPERIENCING MOST RIGHT NOW:

GOALS FOR TODAY:

THINGS THAT CAN WAIT:

HOW I INTEND TO REJUVENATE MY MIND AND BODY TODAY:

- ☐ EXERCISING
- ☐ LISTENING TO MUSIC
- ☐ MEDITATING
- ☐ JOURNALING
- ☐ READING
- ☐ TALKING TO SOMEONE
- ☐ TIME WITH LOVED ONES
- ☐ TIME WITH A PET
- ☐ GRATITUDE/POSITIVE SELF-TALK
- ☐ TIME OUTSIDE
- ☐ DOWNTIME
- ☐ OTHER: ______

EVENING REFLECTION

POOR MY MOOD THIS EVENING GREAT

1 2 3 4 5 6 7 8 9 10

DIFFICULT EMOTIONS THAT I EXPERIENCED TODAY:

MOMENTS OF HAPPINESS/JOY I EXPERIENCED TODAY:

A SELF-PRAISE OR GRATITUDE:

THIS HELPED ME THE MOST TODAY:

SOMETHING I NEED HELP WITH:

MORNING REFLECTION

DATE ___/___/___

HOURS SLEPT: ________

POOR — MY MOOD THIS MORNING — GREAT

1 2 3 4 5 6 7 8 9 10

THOUGHTS I WOKE UP WITH / I WOKE UP FEELING:

THE FEELINGS I'M EXPERIENCING MOST RIGHT NOW:

GOALS FOR TODAY:

THINGS THAT CAN WAIT:

HOW I INTEND TO REJUVENATE MY MIND AND BODY TODAY:

- ☐ EXERCISING
- ☐ LISTENING TO MUSIC
- ☐ MEDITATING
- ☐ JOURNALING
- ☐ READING
- ☐ TALKING TO SOMEONE
- ☐ TIME WITH LOVED ONES
- ☐ TIME WITH A PET
- ☐ GRATITUDE/POSITIVE SELF-TALK
- ☐ TIME OUTSIDE
- ☐ DOWNTIME
- ☐ OTHER: ________

EVENING REFLECTION

POOR — MY MOOD THIS EVENING — GREAT

1 2 3 4 5 6 7 8 9 10

DIFFICULT EMOTIONS THAT I EXPERIENCED TODAY:

MOMENTS OF HAPPINESS/JOY I EXPERIENCED TODAY:

A SELF-PRAISE OR GRATITUDE:

THIS HELPED ME THE MOST TODAY:

SOMETHING I NEED HELP WITH:

MORNING REFLECTION

DATE ___/___/___

HOURS SLEPT: ____________

MY MOOD THIS MORNING

POOR 1 2 3 4 5 6 7 8 9 10 GREAT

THOUGHTS I WOKE UP WITH / I WOKE UP FEELING:

THE FEELINGS I'M EXPERIENCING MOST RIGHT NOW:

GOALS FOR TODAY:

THINGS THAT CAN WAIT:

HOW I INTEND TO REJUVENATE MY MIND AND BODY TODAY:

- ☐ EXERCISING
- ☐ LISTENING TO MUSIC
- ☐ MEDITATING
- ☐ JOURNALING
- ☐ READING
- ☐ TALKING TO SOMEONE
- ☐ TIME WITH LOVED ONES
- ☐ TIME WITH A PET
- ☐ GRATITUDE/POSITIVE SELF-TALK
- ☐ TIME OUTSIDE
- ☐ DOWNTIME
- ☐ OTHER: ____________

EVENING REFLECTION

POOR — MY MOOD THIS EVENING — GREAT

1 2 3 4 5 6 7 8 9 10

DIFFICULT EMOTIONS THAT I EXPERIENCED TODAY:

MOMENTS OF HAPPINESS/JOY I EXPERIENCED TODAY:

A SELF-PRAISE OR GRATITUDE:

THIS HELPED ME THE MOST TODAY:

SOMETHING I NEED HELP WITH:

MORNING REFLECTION

DATE ___/___/___

HOURS SLEPT: ____________

POOR — MY MOOD THIS MORNING — GREAT

1 2 3 4 5 6 7 8 9 10

THOUGHTS I WOKE UP WITH / I WOKE UP FEELING:

THE FEELINGS I'M EXPERIENCING MOST RIGHT NOW:

GOALS FOR TODAY:

THINGS THAT CAN WAIT:

HOW I INTEND TO REJUVENATE MY MIND AND BODY TODAY:

- ☐ EXERCISING
- ☐ LISTENING TO MUSIC
- ☐ MEDITATING
- ☐ JOURNALING
- ☐ READING
- ☐ TALKING TO SOMEONE
- ☐ TIME WITH LOVED ONES
- ☐ TIME WITH A PET
- ☐ GRATITUDE/POSITIVE SELF-TALK
- ☐ TIME OUTSIDE
- ☐ DOWNTIME
- ☐ OTHER: ____________

EVENING REFLECTION

POOR — MY MOOD THIS EVENING — GREAT

1 2 3 4 5 6 7 8 9 10

DIFFICULT EMOTIONS THAT I EXPERIENCED TODAY:

MOMENTS OF HAPPINESS/JOY I EXPERIENCED TODAY:

A SELF-PRAISE OR GRATITUDE:

THIS HELPED ME THE MOST TODAY:

SOMETHING I NEED HELP WITH:

MORNING REFLECTION

DATE ___/___/___

HOURS SLEPT:	POOR			MY MOOD THIS MORNING						GREAT
______	1	2	3	4	5	6	7	8	9	10

THOUGHTS I WOKE UP WITH / I WOKE UP FEELING:

THE FEELINGS I'M EXPERIENCING MOST RIGHT NOW:

GOALS FOR TODAY:

THINGS THAT CAN WAIT:

HOW I INTEND TO REJUVENATE MY MIND AND BODY TODAY:

- ☐ EXERCISING
- ☐ LISTENING TO MUSIC
- ☐ MEDITATING
- ☐ JOURNALING
- ☐ READING
- ☐ TALKING TO SOMEONE
- ☐ TIME WITH LOVED ONES
- ☐ TIME WITH A PET
- ☐ GRATITUDE/POSITIVE SELF-TALK
- ☐ TIME OUTSIDE
- ☐ DOWNTIME
- ☐ OTHER: ______

EVENING REFLECTION

POOR | MY MOOD THIS EVENING | GREAT

1 2 3 4 5 6 7 8 9 10

DIFFICULT EMOTIONS THAT I EXPERIENCED TODAY:

MOMENTS OF HAPPINESS/JOY I EXPERIENCED TODAY:

A SELF-PRAISE OR GRATITUDE:

THIS HELPED ME THE MOST TODAY:

SOMETHING I NEED HELP WITH:

MORNING REFLECTION

DATE ___/___/___

HOURS SLEPT: ______________

MY MOOD THIS MORNING

POOR 1 2 3 4 5 6 7 8 9 10 GREAT

THOUGHTS I WOKE UP WITH / I WOKE UP FEELING:

THE FEELINGS I'M EXPERIENCING MOST RIGHT NOW:

GOALS FOR TODAY:

THINGS THAT CAN WAIT:

HOW I INTEND TO REJUVENATE MY MIND AND BODY TODAY:

- ☐ EXERCISING
- ☐ LISTENING TO MUSIC
- ☐ MEDITATING
- ☐ JOURNALING
- ☐ READING
- ☐ TALKING TO SOMEONE
- ☐ TIME WITH LOVED ONES
- ☐ TIME WITH A PET
- ☐ GRATITUDE/POSITIVE SELF-TALK
- ☐ TIME OUTSIDE
- ☐ DOWNTIME
- ☐ OTHER: ______________

EVENING REFLECTION

POOR MY MOOD THIS EVENING GREAT

1 2 3 4 5 6 7 8 9 10

DIFFICULT EMOTIONS THAT I EXPERIENCED TODAY:

MOMENTS OF HAPPINESS/JOY I EXPERIENCED TODAY:

A SELF-PRAISE OR GRATITUDE:

THIS HELPED ME THE MOST TODAY:

SOMETHING I NEED HELP WITH:

MORNING REFLECTION

DATE ___/___/___

HOURS SLEPT: ____________

MY MOOD THIS MORNING

POOR 1 2 3 4 5 6 7 8 9 10 GREAT

THOUGHTS I WOKE UP WITH / I WOKE UP FEELING:

THE FEELINGS I'M EXPERIENCING MOST RIGHT NOW:

GOALS FOR TODAY:

THINGS THAT CAN WAIT:

HOW I INTEND TO REJUVENATE MY MIND AND BODY TODAY:

- ☐ EXERCISING
- ☐ LISTENING TO MUSIC
- ☐ MEDITATING
- ☐ JOURNALING
- ☐ READING
- ☐ TALKING TO SOMEONE
- ☐ TIME WITH LOVED ONES
- ☐ TIME WITH A PET
- ☐ GRATITUDE/POSITIVE SELF-TALK
- ☐ TIME OUTSIDE
- ☐ DOWNTIME
- ☐ OTHER: ____________

EVENING REFLECTION

POOR MY MOOD THIS EVENING GREAT

1 2 3 4 5 6 7 8 9 10

DIFFICULT EMOTIONS THAT I EXPERIENCED TODAY:

MOMENTS OF HAPPINESS/JOY I EXPERIENCED TODAY:

A SELF-PRAISE OR GRATITUDE:

THIS HELPED ME THE MOST TODAY:

SOMETHING I NEED HELP WITH:

MORNING REFLECTION

DATE ___/___/___

HOURS SLEPT: __________

POOR — MY MOOD THIS MORNING — GREAT

1 2 3 4 5 6 7 8 9 10

THOUGHTS I WOKE UP WITH / I WOKE UP FEELING:

THE FEELINGS I'M EXPERIENCING MOST RIGHT NOW:

GOALS FOR TODAY:

THINGS THAT CAN WAIT:

HOW I INTEND TO REJUVENATE MY MIND AND BODY TODAY:

- ☐ EXERCISING
- ☐ LISTENING TO MUSIC
- ☐ MEDITATING
- ☐ JOURNALING
- ☐ READING
- ☐ TALKING TO SOMEONE
- ☐ TIME WITH LOVED ONES
- ☐ TIME WITH A PET
- ☐ GRATITUDE/POSITIVE SELF-TALK
- ☐ TIME OUTSIDE
- ☐ DOWNTIME
- ☐ OTHER: __________

EVENING REFLECTION

POOR MY MOOD THIS EVENING GREAT

1 2 3 4 5 6 7 8 9 10

DIFFICULT EMOTIONS THAT I EXPERIENCED TODAY:

MOMENTS OF HAPPINESS/JOY I EXPERIENCED TODAY:

A SELF-PRAISE OR GRATITUDE:

THIS HELPED ME THE MOST TODAY:

SOMETHING I NEED HELP WITH:

MORNING REFLECTION

DATE ___/___/___

HOURS SLEPT: ________

MY MOOD THIS MORNING

POOR 1 2 3 4 5 6 7 8 9 10 GREAT

THOUGHTS I WOKE UP WITH / I WOKE UP FEELING:

THE FEELINGS I'M EXPERIENCING MOST RIGHT NOW:

GOALS FOR TODAY:

THINGS THAT CAN WAIT:

HOW I INTEND TO REJUVENATE MY MIND AND BODY TODAY:

- ☐ EXERCISING
- ☐ LISTENING TO MUSIC
- ☐ MEDITATING
- ☐ JOURNALING
- ☐ READING
- ☐ TALKING TO SOMEONE
- ☐ TIME WITH LOVED ONES
- ☐ TIME WITH A PET
- ☐ GRATITUDE/POSITIVE SELF-TALK
- ☐ TIME OUTSIDE
- ☐ DOWNTIME
- ☐ OTHER: ________

EVENING REFLECTION

POOR MY MOOD THIS EVENING GREAT

1 2 3 4 5 6 7 8 9 10

DIFFICULT EMOTIONS THAT I EXPERIENCED TODAY:

MOMENTS OF HAPPINESS/JOY I EXPERIENCED TODAY:

A SELF-PRAISE OR GRATITUDE:

THIS HELPED ME THE MOST TODAY:

SOMETHING I NEED HELP WITH:

MORNING REFLECTION

DATE ___/___/___

HOURS SLEPT: ____________

MY MOOD THIS MORNING

POOR 1 2 3 4 5 6 7 8 9 10 GREAT

THOUGHTS I WOKE UP WITH / I WOKE UP FEELING:

THE FEELINGS I'M EXPERIENCING MOST RIGHT NOW:

GOALS FOR TODAY:

THINGS THAT CAN WAIT:

HOW I INTEND TO REJUVENATE MY MIND AND BODY TODAY:

- ☐ EXERCISING
- ☐ LISTENING TO MUSIC
- ☐ MEDITATING
- ☐ JOURNALING
- ☐ READING
- ☐ TALKING TO SOMEONE
- ☐ TIME WITH LOVED ONES
- ☐ TIME WITH A PET
- ☐ GRATITUDE/POSITIVE SELF-TALK
- ☐ TIME OUTSIDE
- ☐ DOWNTIME
- ☐ OTHER: ____________

EVENING REFLECTION

POOR MY MOOD THIS EVENING GREAT

1 2 3 4 5 6 7 8 9 10

DIFFICULT EMOTIONS THAT I EXPERIENCED TODAY:

MOMENTS OF HAPPINESS/JOY I EXPERIENCED TODAY:

A SELF-PRAISE OR GRATITUDE:

THIS HELPED ME THE MOST TODAY:

SOMETHING I NEED HELP WITH:

MORNING REFLECTION

DATE ___/___/___

HOURS SLEPT: ____________

POOR — MY MOOD THIS MORNING — GREAT

1 2 3 4 5 6 7 8 9 10

THOUGHTS I WOKE UP WITH / I WOKE UP FEELING:

THE FEELINGS I'M EXPERIENCING MOST RIGHT NOW:

GOALS FOR TODAY:

THINGS THAT CAN WAIT:

HOW I INTEND TO REJUVENATE MY MIND AND BODY TODAY:

- ☐ EXERCISING
- ☐ LISTENING TO MUSIC
- ☐ MEDITATING
- ☐ JOURNALING
- ☐ READING
- ☐ TALKING TO SOMEONE
- ☐ TIME WITH LOVED ONES
- ☐ TIME WITH A PET
- ☐ GRATITUDE/POSITIVE SELF-TALK
- ☐ TIME OUTSIDE
- ☐ DOWNTIME
- ☐ OTHER: ____________

EVENING REFLECTION

POOR MY MOOD THIS EVENING GREAT

1 2 3 4 5 6 7 8 9 10

DIFFICULT EMOTIONS THAT I EXPERIENCED TODAY:

MOMENTS OF HAPPINESS/JOY I EXPERIENCED TODAY:

A SELF-PRAISE OR GRATITUDE:

THIS HELPED ME THE MOST TODAY:

SOMETHING I NEED HELP WITH:

MORNING REFLECTION

DATE ___/___/___

HOURS SLEPT: ______

POOR — MY MOOD THIS MORNING — GREAT

1 2 3 4 5 6 7 8 9 10

THOUGHTS I WOKE UP WITH / I WOKE UP FEELING:

THE FEELINGS I'M EXPERIENCING MOST RIGHT NOW:

GOALS FOR TODAY:

THINGS THAT CAN WAIT:

HOW I INTEND TO REJUVENATE MY MIND AND BODY TODAY:

- ☐ EXERCISING
- ☐ LISTENING TO MUSIC
- ☐ MEDITATING
- ☐ JOURNALING
- ☐ READING
- ☐ TALKING TO SOMEONE
- ☐ TIME WITH LOVED ONES
- ☐ TIME WITH A PET
- ☐ GRATITUDE/POSITIVE SELF-TALK
- ☐ TIME OUTSIDE
- ☐ DOWNTIME
- ☐ OTHER: ______

EVENING REFLECTION

POOR — MY MOOD THIS EVENING — GREAT

1 2 3 4 5 6 7 8 9 10

DIFFICULT EMOTIONS THAT I EXPERIENCED TODAY:

MOMENTS OF HAPPINESS/JOY I EXPERIENCED TODAY:

A SELF-PRAISE OR GRATITUDE:

THIS HELPED ME THE MOST TODAY:

SOMETHING I NEED HELP WITH:

MORNING REFLECTION

DATE ___/___/___

HOURS SLEPT: ______

MY MOOD THIS MORNING

POOR 1 2 3 4 5 6 7 8 9 10 GREAT

THOUGHTS I WOKE UP WITH / I WOKE UP FEELING:

THE FEELINGS I'M EXPERIENCING MOST RIGHT NOW:

GOALS FOR TODAY:

THINGS THAT CAN WAIT:

HOW I INTEND TO REJUVENATE MY MIND AND BODY TODAY:

- ☐ EXERCISING
- ☐ LISTENING TO MUSIC
- ☐ MEDITATING
- ☐ JOURNALING
- ☐ READING
- ☐ TALKING TO SOMEONE
- ☐ TIME WITH LOVED ONES
- ☐ TIME WITH A PET
- ☐ GRATITUDE/POSITIVE SELF-TALK
- ☐ TIME OUTSIDE
- ☐ DOWNTIME
- ☐ OTHER: ______

EVENING REFLECTION

POOR MY MOOD THIS EVENING GREAT

1 2 3 4 5 6 7 8 9 10

DIFFICULT EMOTIONS THAT I EXPERIENCED TODAY:

MOMENTS OF HAPPINESS/JOY I EXPERIENCED TODAY:

A SELF-PRAISE OR GRATITUDE:

THIS HELPED ME THE MOST TODAY:

SOMETHING I NEED HELP WITH:

MORNING REFLECTION

DATE ___/___/___

HOURS SLEPT: ____________

MY MOOD THIS MORNING

POOR 1 2 3 4 5 6 7 8 9 10 GREAT

THOUGHTS I WOKE UP WITH / I WOKE UP FEELING:

THE FEELINGS I'M EXPERIENCING MOST RIGHT NOW:

GOALS FOR TODAY:

THINGS THAT CAN WAIT:

HOW I INTEND TO REJUVENATE MY MIND AND BODY TODAY:

- ☐ EXERCISING
- ☐ LISTENING TO MUSIC
- ☐ MEDITATING
- ☐ JOURNALING
- ☐ READING
- ☐ TALKING TO SOMEONE
- ☐ TIME WITH LOVED ONES
- ☐ TIME WITH A PET
- ☐ GRATITUDE/POSITIVE SELF-TALK
- ☐ TIME OUTSIDE
- ☐ DOWNTIME
- ☐ OTHER: ____________

EVENING REFLECTION

POOR MY MOOD THIS EVENING GREAT

1 2 3 4 5 6 7 8 9 10

DIFFICULT EMOTIONS THAT I EXPERIENCED TODAY:

MOMENTS OF HAPPINESS/JOY I EXPERIENCED TODAY:

A SELF-PRAISE OR GRATITUDE:

THIS HELPED ME THE MOST TODAY:

SOMETHING I NEED HELP WITH:

MORNING REFLECTION

DATE ___/___/___

HOURS SLEPT: ______________

MY MOOD THIS MORNING

POOR 1 2 3 4 5 6 7 8 9 10 GREAT

THOUGHTS I WOKE UP WITH / I WOKE UP FEELING:

THE FEELINGS I'M EXPERIENCING MOST RIGHT NOW:

GOALS FOR TODAY:

THINGS THAT CAN WAIT:

HOW I INTEND TO REJUVENATE MY MIND AND BODY TODAY:

- ☐ EXERCISING
- ☐ LISTENING TO MUSIC
- ☐ MEDITATING
- ☐ JOURNALING
- ☐ READING
- ☐ TALKING TO SOMEONE
- ☐ TIME WITH LOVED ONES
- ☐ TIME WITH A PET
- ☐ GRATITUDE/POSITIVE SELF-TALK
- ☐ TIME OUTSIDE
- ☐ DOWNTIME
- ☐ OTHER: ______________

EVENING REFLECTION

POOR MY MOOD THIS EVENING GREAT

1 2 3 4 5 6 7 8 9 10

DIFFICULT EMOTIONS THAT I EXPERIENCED TODAY:

MOMENTS OF HAPPINESS/JOY I EXPERIENCED TODAY:

A SELF-PRAISE OR GRATITUDE:

THIS HELPED ME THE MOST TODAY:

SOMETHING I NEED HELP WITH:

MORNING REFLECTION

DATE ___/___/___

HOURS SLEPT: ________

MY MOOD THIS MORNING

POOR 1 2 3 4 5 6 7 8 9 10 GREAT

THOUGHTS I WOKE UP WITH / I WOKE UP FEELING:

THE FEELINGS I'M EXPERIENCING MOST RIGHT NOW:

GOALS FOR TODAY:

THINGS THAT CAN WAIT:

HOW I INTEND TO REJUVENATE MY MIND AND BODY TODAY:

- ☐ EXERCISING
- ☐ LISTENING TO MUSIC
- ☐ MEDITATING
- ☐ JOURNALING
- ☐ READING
- ☐ TALKING TO SOMEONE
- ☐ TIME WITH LOVED ONES
- ☐ TIME WITH A PET
- ☐ GRATITUDE/POSITIVE SELF-TALK
- ☐ TIME OUTSIDE
- ☐ DOWNTIME
- ☐ OTHER: ________

EVENING REFLECTION

POOR MY MOOD THIS EVENING GREAT

1 2 3 4 5 6 7 8 9 10

DIFFICULT EMOTIONS THAT I EXPERIENCED TODAY:

MOMENTS OF HAPPINESS/JOY I EXPERIENCED TODAY:

A SELF-PRAISE OR GRATITUDE:

THIS HELPED ME THE MOST TODAY:

SOMETHING I NEED HELP WITH:

MORNING REFLECTION

DATE ___/___/___

HOURS SLEPT: ____________

MY MOOD THIS MORNING

POOR 1 2 3 4 5 6 7 8 9 10 GREAT

THOUGHTS I WOKE UP WITH / I WOKE UP FEELING:

THE FEELINGS I'M EXPERIENCING MOST RIGHT NOW:

GOALS FOR TODAY:

THINGS THAT CAN WAIT:

HOW I INTEND TO REJUVENATE MY MIND AND BODY TODAY:

- ☐ EXERCISING
- ☐ LISTENING TO MUSIC
- ☐ MEDITATING
- ☐ JOURNALING
- ☐ READING
- ☐ TALKING TO SOMEONE
- ☐ TIME WITH LOVED ONES
- ☐ TIME WITH A PET
- ☐ GRATITUDE/POSITIVE SELF-TALK
- ☐ TIME OUTSIDE
- ☐ DOWNTIME
- ☐ OTHER: ____________

EVENING REFLECTION

POOR — MY MOOD THIS EVENING — GREAT

1 2 3 4 5 6 7 8 9 10

DIFFICULT EMOTIONS THAT I EXPERIENCED TODAY:

MOMENTS OF HAPPINESS/JOY I EXPERIENCED TODAY:

A SELF-PRAISE OR GRATITUDE:

THIS HELPED ME THE MOST TODAY:

SOMETHING I NEED HELP WITH:

MORNING REFLECTION

DATE ___/___/___

HOURS SLEPT: ________

POOR — MY MOOD THIS MORNING — GREAT

1 2 3 4 5 6 7 8 9 10

THOUGHTS I WOKE UP WITH / I WOKE UP FEELING:

THE FEELINGS I'M EXPERIENCING MOST RIGHT NOW:

GOALS FOR TODAY:

THINGS THAT CAN WAIT:

HOW I INTEND TO REJUVENATE MY MIND AND BODY TODAY:

- ☐ EXERCISING
- ☐ LISTENING TO MUSIC
- ☐ MEDITATING
- ☐ JOURNALING
- ☐ READING
- ☐ TALKING TO SOMEONE
- ☐ TIME WITH LOVED ONES
- ☐ TIME WITH A PET
- ☐ GRATITUDE/POSITIVE SELF-TALK
- ☐ TIME OUTSIDE
- ☐ DOWNTIME
- ☐ OTHER: ________

EVENING REFLECTION

POOR MY MOOD THIS EVENING GREAT

1 2 3 4 5 6 7 8 9 10

DIFFICULT EMOTIONS THAT I EXPERIENCED TODAY:

MOMENTS OF HAPPINESS/JOY I EXPERIENCED TODAY:

A SELF-PRAISE OR GRATITUDE:

THIS HELPED ME THE MOST TODAY:

SOMETHING I NEED HELP WITH:

MORNING REFLECTION

DATE ___/___/___

HOURS SLEPT: ______________

POOR — MY MOOD THIS MORNING — GREAT

1 2 3 4 5 6 7 8 9 10

THOUGHTS I WOKE UP WITH / I WOKE UP FEELING:

THE FEELINGS I'M EXPERIENCING MOST RIGHT NOW:

GOALS FOR TODAY:

THINGS THAT CAN WAIT:

HOW I INTEND TO REJUVENATE MY MIND AND BODY TODAY:

- ☐ EXERCISING
- ☐ LISTENING TO MUSIC
- ☐ MEDITATING
- ☐ JOURNALING
- ☐ READING
- ☐ TALKING TO SOMEONE
- ☐ TIME WITH LOVED ONES
- ☐ TIME WITH A PET
- ☐ GRATITUDE/POSITIVE SELF-TALK
- ☐ TIME OUTSIDE
- ☐ DOWNTIME
- ☐ OTHER: ______________

EVENING REFLECTION

POOR MY MOOD THIS EVENING GREAT

1 2 3 4 5 6 7 8 9 10

DIFFICULT EMOTIONS THAT I EXPERIENCED TODAY:

MOMENTS OF HAPPINESS/JOY I EXPERIENCED TODAY:

A SELF-PRAISE OR GRATITUDE:

THIS HELPED ME THE MOST TODAY:

SOMETHING I NEED HELP WITH:

MORNING REFLECTION

DATE ___/___/___

HOURS SLEPT: ____________

MY MOOD THIS MORNING

POOR 1 2 3 4 5 6 7 8 9 10 GREAT

THOUGHTS I WOKE UP WITH / I WOKE UP FEELING:

THE FEELINGS I'M EXPERIENCING MOST RIGHT NOW:

GOALS FOR TODAY:

THINGS THAT CAN WAIT:

HOW I INTEND TO REJUVENATE MY MIND AND BODY TODAY:

- ☐ EXERCISING
- ☐ LISTENING TO MUSIC
- ☐ MEDITATING
- ☐ JOURNALING
- ☐ READING
- ☐ TALKING TO SOMEONE
- ☐ TIME WITH LOVED ONES
- ☐ TIME WITH A PET
- ☐ GRATITUDE/POSITIVE SELF-TALK
- ☐ TIME OUTSIDE
- ☐ DOWNTIME
- ☐ OTHER: ____________

EVENING REFLECTION

POOR | MY MOOD THIS EVENING | GREAT

1 2 3 4 5 6 7 8 9 10

DIFFICULT EMOTIONS THAT I EXPERIENCED TODAY:

MOMENTS OF HAPPINESS/JOY I EXPERIENCED TODAY:

A SELF-PRAISE OR GRATITUDE:

THIS HELPED ME THE MOST TODAY:

SOMETHING I NEED HELP WITH:

MORNING REFLECTION

DATE ___/___/___

HOURS SLEPT: ____________

MY MOOD THIS MORNING

POOR 1 2 3 4 5 6 7 8 9 10 GREAT

THOUGHTS I WOKE UP WITH / I WOKE UP FEELING:

THE FEELINGS I'M EXPERIENCING MOST RIGHT NOW:

GOALS FOR TODAY:

THINGS THAT CAN WAIT:

HOW I INTEND TO REJUVENATE MY MIND AND BODY TODAY:

- ☐ EXERCISING
- ☐ LISTENING TO MUSIC
- ☐ MEDITATING
- ☐ JOURNALING
- ☐ READING
- ☐ TALKING TO SOMEONE
- ☐ TIME WITH LOVED ONES
- ☐ TIME WITH A PET
- ☐ GRATITUDE/POSITIVE SELF-TALK
- ☐ TIME OUTSIDE
- ☐ DOWNTIME
- ☐ OTHER: ____________

EVENING REFLECTION

POOR MY MOOD THIS EVENING GREAT

1 2 3 4 5 6 7 8 9 10

DIFFICULT EMOTIONS THAT I EXPERIENCED TODAY:

MOMENTS OF HAPPINESS/JOY I EXPERIENCED TODAY:

A SELF-PRAISE OR GRATITUDE:

THIS HELPED ME THE MOST TODAY:

SOMETHING I NEED HELP WITH:

MORNING REFLECTION

DATE ___/___/___

HOURS SLEPT: ________

MY MOOD THIS MORNING

POOR 1 2 3 4 5 6 7 8 9 10 GREAT

THOUGHTS I WOKE UP WITH / I WOKE UP FEELING:

THE FEELINGS I'M EXPERIENCING MOST RIGHT NOW:

GOALS FOR TODAY:

THINGS THAT CAN WAIT:

HOW I INTEND TO REJUVENATE MY MIND AND BODY TODAY:

- ☐ EXERCISING
- ☐ LISTENING TO MUSIC
- ☐ MEDITATING
- ☐ JOURNALING
- ☐ READING
- ☐ TALKING TO SOMEONE
- ☐ TIME WITH LOVED ONES
- ☐ TIME WITH A PET
- ☐ GRATITUDE/POSITIVE SELF-TALK
- ☐ TIME OUTSIDE
- ☐ DOWNTIME
- ☐ OTHER: ________

EVENING REFLECTION

POOR | MY MOOD THIS EVENING | GREAT

1 2 3 4 5 6 7 8 9 10

DIFFICULT EMOTIONS THAT I EXPERIENCED TODAY:

MOMENTS OF HAPPINESS/JOY I EXPERIENCED TODAY:

A SELF-PRAISE OR GRATITUDE:

THIS HELPED ME THE MOST TODAY:

SOMETHING I NEED HELP WITH:

MORNING REFLECTION

DATE ___/___/___

HOURS SLEPT: ______________

MY MOOD THIS MORNING

POOR 1 2 3 4 5 6 7 8 9 10 GREAT

THOUGHTS I WOKE UP WITH / I WOKE UP FEELING:

THE FEELINGS I'M EXPERIENCING MOST RIGHT NOW:

GOALS FOR TODAY:

THINGS THAT CAN WAIT:

HOW I INTEND TO REJUVENATE MY MIND AND BODY TODAY:

- ☐ EXERCISING
- ☐ LISTENING TO MUSIC
- ☐ MEDITATING
- ☐ JOURNALING
- ☐ READING
- ☐ TALKING TO SOMEONE
- ☐ TIME WITH LOVED ONES
- ☐ TIME WITH A PET
- ☐ GRATITUDE/POSITIVE SELF-TALK
- ☐ TIME OUTSIDE
- ☐ DOWNTIME
- ☐ OTHER: ______________

EVENING REFLECTION

POOR — MY MOOD THIS EVENING — GREAT

1 2 3 4 5 6 7 8 9 10

DIFFICULT EMOTIONS THAT I EXPERIENCED TODAY:

MOMENTS OF HAPPINESS/JOY I EXPERIENCED TODAY:

A SELF-PRAISE OR GRATITUDE:

THIS HELPED ME THE MOST TODAY:

SOMETHING I NEED HELP WITH:

MORNING REFLECTION

DATE ___/___/___

HOURS SLEPT: ______

MY MOOD THIS MORNING

POOR 1 2 3 4 5 6 7 8 9 10 GREAT

THOUGHTS I WOKE UP WITH / I WOKE UP FEELING:

______

______

______

______

THE FEELINGS I'M EXPERIENCING MOST RIGHT NOW:

______

______

______

______

GOALS FOR TODAY:

______

______

______

THINGS THAT CAN WAIT:

______

______

______

HOW I INTEND TO REJUVENATE MY MIND AND BODY TODAY:

- ☐ EXERCISING
- ☐ LISTENING TO MUSIC
- ☐ MEDITATING
- ☐ JOURNALING
- ☐ READING
- ☐ TALKING TO SOMEONE
- ☐ TIME WITH LOVED ONES
- ☐ TIME WITH A PET
- ☐ GRATITUDE/POSITIVE SELF-TALK
- ☐ TIME OUTSIDE
- ☐ DOWNTIME
- ☐ OTHER: ______

EVENING REFLECTION

POOR MY MOOD THIS EVENING GREAT

1 2 3 4 5 6 7 8 9 10

DIFFICULT EMOTIONS THAT I EXPERIENCED TODAY:

MOMENTS OF HAPPINESS/JOY I EXPERIENCED TODAY:

A SELF-PRAISE OR GRATITUDE:

THIS HELPED ME THE MOST TODAY:

SOMETHING I NEED HELP WITH:

MORNING REFLECTION

DATE ___/___/___

HOURS SLEPT: ____________

MY MOOD THIS MORNING

POOR 1 2 3 4 5 6 7 8 9 10 GREAT

THOUGHTS I WOKE UP WITH / I WOKE UP FEELING:

THE FEELINGS I'M EXPERIENCING MOST RIGHT NOW:

GOALS FOR TODAY:

THINGS THAT CAN WAIT:

HOW I INTEND TO REJUVENATE MY MIND AND BODY TODAY:

- ☐ EXERCISING
- ☐ LISTENING TO MUSIC
- ☐ MEDITATING
- ☐ JOURNALING
- ☐ READING
- ☐ TALKING TO SOMEONE
- ☐ TIME WITH LOVED ONES
- ☐ TIME WITH A PET
- ☐ GRATITUDE/POSITIVE SELF-TALK
- ☐ TIME OUTSIDE
- ☐ DOWNTIME
- ☐ OTHER: ____________

EVENING REFLECTION

POOR MY MOOD THIS EVENING GREAT

1 2 3 4 5 6 7 8 9 10

DIFFICULT EMOTIONS THAT I EXPERIENCED TODAY:

MOMENTS OF HAPPINESS/JOY I EXPERIENCED TODAY:

A SELF-PRAISE OR GRATITUDE:

THIS HELPED ME THE MOST TODAY:

SOMETHING I NEED HELP WITH:

MORNING REFLECTION

DATE ___/___/___

HOURS SLEPT: ____________

MY MOOD THIS MORNING

POOR 1 2 3 4 5 6 7 8 9 10 GREAT

THOUGHTS I WOKE UP WITH / I WOKE UP FEELING:

THE FEELINGS I'M EXPERIENCING MOST RIGHT NOW:

GOALS FOR TODAY:

THINGS THAT CAN WAIT:

HOW I INTEND TO REJUVENATE MY MIND AND BODY TODAY:

- ☐ EXERCISING
- ☐ LISTENING TO MUSIC
- ☐ MEDITATING
- ☐ JOURNALING
- ☐ READING
- ☐ TALKING TO SOMEONE
- ☐ TIME WITH LOVED ONES
- ☐ TIME WITH A PET
- ☐ GRATITUDE/POSITIVE SELF-TALK
- ☐ TIME OUTSIDE
- ☐ DOWNTIME
- ☐ OTHER: ____________

EVENING REFLECTION

POOR — MY MOOD THIS EVENING — GREAT

1 2 3 4 5 6 7 8 9 10

DIFFICULT EMOTIONS THAT I EXPERIENCED TODAY:

MOMENTS OF HAPPINESS/JOY I EXPERIENCED TODAY:

A SELF-PRAISE OR GRATITUDE:

THIS HELPED ME THE MOST TODAY:

SOMETHING I NEED HELP WITH:

MORNING REFLECTION

DATE ___/___/___

HOURS SLEPT: ______________

MY MOOD THIS MORNING

POOR 1 2 3 4 5 6 7 8 9 10 GREAT

THOUGHTS I WOKE UP WITH / I WOKE UP FEELING:

THE FEELINGS I'M EXPERIENCING MOST RIGHT NOW:

GOALS FOR TODAY:

THINGS THAT CAN WAIT:

HOW I INTEND TO REJUVENATE MY MIND AND BODY TODAY:

- ☐ EXERCISING
- ☐ LISTENING TO MUSIC
- ☐ MEDITATING
- ☐ JOURNALING
- ☐ READING
- ☐ TALKING TO SOMEONE
- ☐ TIME WITH LOVED ONES
- ☐ TIME WITH A PET
- ☐ GRATITUDE/POSITIVE SELF-TALK
- ☐ TIME OUTSIDE
- ☐ DOWNTIME
- ☐ OTHER: ______________

EVENING REFLECTION

POOR MY MOOD THIS EVENING GREAT

1 2 3 4 5 6 7 8 9 10

DIFFICULT EMOTIONS THAT I EXPERIENCED TODAY:

MOMENTS OF HAPPINESS/JOY I EXPERIENCED TODAY:

A SELF-PRAISE OR GRATITUDE:

THIS HELPED ME THE MOST TODAY:

SOMETHING I NEED HELP WITH:

MORNING REFLECTION

DATE ___/___/___

HOURS SLEPT: ____________

MY MOOD THIS MORNING

POOR 1 2 3 4 5 6 7 8 9 10 GREAT

THOUGHTS I WOKE UP WITH / I WOKE UP FEELING:

THE FEELINGS I'M EXPERIENCING MOST RIGHT NOW:

GOALS FOR TODAY:

THINGS THAT CAN WAIT:

HOW I INTEND TO REJUVENATE MY MIND AND BODY TODAY:

- ☐ EXERCISING
- ☐ LISTENING TO MUSIC
- ☐ MEDITATING
- ☐ JOURNALING
- ☐ READING
- ☐ TALKING TO SOMEONE
- ☐ TIME WITH LOVED ONES
- ☐ TIME WITH A PET
- ☐ GRATITUDE/POSITIVE SELF-TALK
- ☐ TIME OUTSIDE
- ☐ DOWNTIME
- ☐ OTHER: ____________

EVENING REFLECTION

POOR MY MOOD THIS EVENING GREAT

1 2 3 4 5 6 7 8 9 10

DIFFICULT EMOTIONS THAT I EXPERIENCED TODAY:

MOMENTS OF HAPPINESS/JOY I EXPERIENCED TODAY:

A SELF-PRAISE OR GRATITUDE:

THIS HELPED ME THE MOST TODAY:

SOMETHING I NEED HELP WITH:

MORNING REFLECTION

DATE ___/___/___

HOURS SLEPT: ____________

MY MOOD THIS MORNING

POOR 1 2 3 4 5 6 7 8 9 10 GREAT

THOUGHTS I WOKE UP WITH / I WOKE UP FEELING:

THE FEELINGS I'M EXPERIENCING MOST RIGHT NOW:

GOALS FOR TODAY:

THINGS THAT CAN WAIT:

HOW I INTEND TO REJUVENATE MY MIND AND BODY TODAY:

- ☐ EXERCISING
- ☐ LISTENING TO MUSIC
- ☐ MEDITATING
- ☐ JOURNALING
- ☐ READING
- ☐ TALKING TO SOMEONE
- ☐ TIME WITH LOVED ONES
- ☐ TIME WITH A PET
- ☐ GRATITUDE/POSITIVE SELF-TALK
- ☐ TIME OUTSIDE
- ☐ DOWNTIME
- ☐ OTHER: ____________

EVENING REFLECTION

POOR MY MOOD THIS EVENING GREAT

1 2 3 4 5 6 7 8 9 10

DIFFICULT EMOTIONS THAT I EXPERIENCED TODAY:

MOMENTS OF HAPPINESS/JOY I EXPERIENCED TODAY:

A SELF-PRAISE OR GRATITUDE:

THIS HELPED ME THE MOST TODAY:

SOMETHING I NEED HELP WITH:

MORNING REFLECTION

DATE ___/___/___

HOURS SLEPT: ______________

MY MOOD THIS MORNING

POOR 1 2 3 4 5 6 7 8 9 10 GREAT

THOUGHTS I WOKE UP WITH / I WOKE UP FEELING:

____
____
____
____

THE FEELINGS I'M EXPERIENCING MOST RIGHT NOW:

____
____
____
____

GOALS FOR TODAY:

____
____
____

THINGS THAT CAN WAIT:

____
____
____

HOW I INTEND TO REJUVENATE MY MIND AND BODY TODAY:

- ☐ EXERCISING
- ☐ LISTENING TO MUSIC
- ☐ MEDITATING
- ☐ JOURNALING
- ☐ READING
- ☐ TALKING TO SOMEONE
- ☐ TIME WITH LOVED ONES
- ☐ TIME WITH A PET
- ☐ GRATITUDE/POSITIVE SELF-TALK
- ☐ TIME OUTSIDE
- ☐ DOWNTIME
- ☐ OTHER: ______________

EVENING REFLECTION

POOR MY MOOD THIS EVENING GREAT

1 2 3 4 5 6 7 8 9 10

DIFFICULT EMOTIONS THAT I EXPERIENCED TODAY:

MOMENTS OF HAPPINESS/JOY I EXPERIENCED TODAY:

A SELF-PRAISE OR GRATITUDE:

THIS HELPED ME THE MOST TODAY:

SOMETHING I NEED HELP WITH:

MORNING REFLECTION

DATE ___/___/___

HOURS SLEPT: ______

MY MOOD THIS MORNING

POOR 1 2 3 4 5 6 7 8 9 10 GREAT

THOUGHTS I WOKE UP WITH / I WOKE UP FEELING:

THE FEELINGS I'M EXPERIENCING MOST RIGHT NOW:

GOALS FOR TODAY:

THINGS THAT CAN WAIT:

HOW I INTEND TO REJUVENATE MY MIND AND BODY TODAY:

- ☐ EXERCISING
- ☐ LISTENING TO MUSIC
- ☐ MEDITATING
- ☐ JOURNALING
- ☐ READING
- ☐ TALKING TO SOMEONE
- ☐ TIME WITH LOVED ONES
- ☐ TIME WITH A PET
- ☐ GRATITUDE/POSITIVE SELF-TALK
- ☐ TIME OUTSIDE
- ☐ DOWNTIME
- ☐ OTHER: ______

EVENING REFLECTION

POOR MY MOOD THIS EVENING GREAT

1 2 3 4 5 6 7 8 9 10

DIFFICULT EMOTIONS THAT I EXPERIENCED TODAY:

MOMENTS OF HAPPINESS/JOY I EXPERIENCED TODAY:

A SELF-PRAISE OR GRATITUDE:

THIS HELPED ME THE MOST TODAY:

SOMETHING I NEED HELP WITH:

MORNING REFLECTION

DATE ___/___/___

HOURS SLEPT: ___________

POOR — MY MOOD THIS MORNING — GREAT

1 2 3 4 5 6 7 8 9 10

THOUGHTS I WOKE UP WITH / I WOKE UP FEELING:

THE FEELINGS I'M EXPERIENCING MOST RIGHT NOW:

GOALS FOR TODAY:

THINGS THAT CAN WAIT:

HOW I INTEND TO REJUVENATE MY MIND AND BODY TODAY:

- ☐ EXERCISING
- ☐ LISTENING TO MUSIC
- ☐ MEDITATING
- ☐ JOURNALING
- ☐ READING
- ☐ TALKING TO SOMEONE
- ☐ TIME WITH LOVED ONES
- ☐ TIME WITH A PET
- ☐ GRATITUDE/POSITIVE SELF-TALK
- ☐ TIME OUTSIDE
- ☐ DOWNTIME
- ☐ OTHER: ___________

EVENING REFLECTION

POOR MY MOOD THIS EVENING GREAT

1 2 3 4 5 6 7 8 9 10

DIFFICULT EMOTIONS THAT I EXPERIENCED TODAY:

MOMENTS OF HAPPINESS/JOY I EXPERIENCED TODAY:

A SELF-PRAISE OR GRATITUDE:

THIS HELPED ME THE MOST TODAY:

SOMETHING I NEED HELP WITH:

MORNING REFLECTION

DATE ___/___/___

HOURS SLEPT: ______________

MY MOOD THIS MORNING

POOR 1 2 3 4 5 6 7 8 9 10 GREAT

THOUGHTS I WOKE UP WITH / I WOKE UP FEELING:

____

____

____

____

THE FEELINGS I'M EXPERIENCING MOST RIGHT NOW:

____

____

____

____

GOALS FOR TODAY:

____

____

____

THINGS THAT CAN WAIT:

____

____

____

HOW I INTEND TO REJUVENATE MY MIND AND BODY TODAY:

- ☐ EXERCISING
- ☐ LISTENING TO MUSIC
- ☐ MEDITATING
- ☐ JOURNALING
- ☐ READING
- ☐ TALKING TO SOMEONE
- ☐ TIME WITH LOVED ONES
- ☐ TIME WITH A PET
- ☐ GRATITUDE/POSITIVE SELF-TALK
- ☐ TIME OUTSIDE
- ☐ DOWNTIME
- ☐ OTHER: ______________

EVENING REFLECTION

POOR MY MOOD THIS EVENING GREAT

1 2 3 4 5 6 7 8 9 10

DIFFICULT EMOTIONS THAT I EXPERIENCED TODAY:

MOMENTS OF HAPPINESS/JOY I EXPERIENCED TODAY:

A SELF-PRAISE OR GRATITUDE:

THIS HELPED ME THE MOST TODAY:

SOMETHING I NEED HELP WITH:

MORNING REFLECTION

DATE ___/___/___

HOURS SLEPT: ______________

MY MOOD THIS MORNING

POOR 1 2 3 4 5 6 7 8 9 10 GREAT

THOUGHTS I WOKE UP WITH / I WOKE UP FEELING:

THE FEELINGS I'M EXPERIENCING MOST RIGHT NOW:

GOALS FOR TODAY:

THINGS THAT CAN WAIT:

HOW I INTEND TO REJUVENATE MY MIND AND BODY TODAY:

- ☐ EXERCISING
- ☐ LISTENING TO MUSIC
- ☐ MEDITATING
- ☐ JOURNALING
- ☐ READING
- ☐ TALKING TO SOMEONE
- ☐ TIME WITH LOVED ONES
- ☐ TIME WITH A PET
- ☐ GRATITUDE/POSITIVE SELF-TALK
- ☐ TIME OUTSIDE
- ☐ DOWNTIME
- ☐ OTHER: ______________

EVENING REFLECTION

POOR MY MOOD THIS EVENING GREAT

1 2 3 4 5 6 7 8 9 10

DIFFICULT EMOTIONS THAT I EXPERIENCED TODAY:

MOMENTS OF HAPPINESS/JOY I EXPERIENCED TODAY:

A SELF-PRAISE OR GRATITUDE:

THIS HELPED ME THE MOST TODAY:

SOMETHING I NEED HELP WITH:

MORNING REFLECTION

DATE ___/___/___

HOURS SLEPT: ____________

MY MOOD THIS MORNING

POOR 1 2 3 4 5 6 7 8 9 10 GREAT

THOUGHTS I WOKE UP WITH / I WOKE UP FEELING:

THE FEELINGS I'M EXPERIENCING MOST RIGHT NOW:

GOALS FOR TODAY:

THINGS THAT CAN WAIT:

HOW I INTEND TO REJUVENATE MY MIND AND BODY TODAY:

- ☐ EXERCISING
- ☐ LISTENING TO MUSIC
- ☐ MEDITATING
- ☐ JOURNALING
- ☐ READING
- ☐ TALKING TO SOMEONE
- ☐ TIME WITH LOVED ONES
- ☐ TIME WITH A PET
- ☐ GRATITUDE/POSITIVE SELF-TALK
- ☐ TIME OUTSIDE
- ☐ DOWNTIME
- ☐ OTHER: ____________

EVENING REFLECTION

POOR MY MOOD THIS EVENING GREAT

1 2 3 4 5 6 7 8 9 10

DIFFICULT EMOTIONS THAT I EXPERIENCED TODAY:

MOMENTS OF HAPPINESS/JOY I EXPERIENCED TODAY:

A SELF-PRAISE OR GRATITUDE:

THIS HELPED ME THE MOST TODAY:

SOMETHING I NEED HELP WITH:

MORNING REFLECTION

DATE ___/___/___

HOURS SLEPT: ____________

MY MOOD THIS MORNING

POOR 1 2 3 4 5 6 7 8 9 10 GREAT

THOUGHTS I WOKE UP WITH / I WOKE UP FEELING:

THE FEELINGS I'M EXPERIENCING MOST RIGHT NOW:

GOALS FOR TODAY:

THINGS THAT CAN WAIT:

HOW I INTEND TO REJUVENATE MY MIND AND BODY TODAY:

- [ ] EXERCISING
- [ ] LISTENING TO MUSIC
- [ ] MEDITATING
- [ ] JOURNALING
- [ ] READING
- [ ] TALKING TO SOMEONE
- [ ] TIME WITH LOVED ONES
- [ ] TIME WITH A PET
- [ ] GRATITUDE/POSITIVE SELF-TALK
- [ ] TIME OUTSIDE
- [ ] DOWNTIME
- [ ] OTHER: ____________

EVENING REFLECTION

POOR MY MOOD THIS EVENING GREAT

1 2 3 4 5 6 7 8 9 10

DIFFICULT EMOTIONS THAT I EXPERIENCED TODAY:

MOMENTS OF HAPPINESS/JOY I EXPERIENCED TODAY:

A SELF-PRAISE OR GRATITUDE:

THIS HELPED ME THE MOST TODAY:

SOMETHING I NEED HELP WITH:

MORNING REFLECTION

DATE ___/___/___

HOURS SLEPT: ____________

MY MOOD THIS MORNING

POOR 1 2 3 4 5 6 7 8 9 10 GREAT

THOUGHTS I WOKE UP WITH / I WOKE UP FEELING:

THE FEELINGS I'M EXPERIENCING MOST RIGHT NOW:

GOALS FOR TODAY:

THINGS THAT CAN WAIT:

HOW I INTEND TO REJUVENATE MY MIND AND BODY TODAY:

- ☐ EXERCISING
- ☐ LISTENING TO MUSIC
- ☐ MEDITATING
- ☐ JOURNALING
- ☐ READING
- ☐ TALKING TO SOMEONE
- ☐ TIME WITH LOVED ONES
- ☐ TIME WITH A PET
- ☐ GRATITUDE/POSITIVE SELF-TALK
- ☐ TIME OUTSIDE
- ☐ DOWNTIME
- ☐ OTHER: ____________

EVENING REFLECTION

POOR MY MOOD THIS EVENING GREAT

1 2 3 4 5 6 7 8 9 10

DIFFICULT EMOTIONS THAT I EXPERIENCED TODAY:

MOMENTS OF HAPPINESS/JOY I EXPERIENCED TODAY:

A SELF-PRAISE OR GRATITUDE:

THIS HELPED ME THE MOST TODAY:

SOMETHING I NEED HELP WITH:

MORNING REFLECTION

DATE ___/___/___

HOURS SLEPT: ____________

MY MOOD THIS MORNING

POOR 1 2 3 4 5 6 7 8 9 10 GREAT

THOUGHTS I WOKE UP WITH / I WOKE UP FEELING:

THE FEELINGS I'M EXPERIENCING MOST RIGHT NOW:

GOALS FOR TODAY:

THINGS THAT CAN WAIT:

HOW I INTEND TO REJUVENATE MY MIND AND BODY TODAY:

- [ ] EXERCISING
- [ ] LISTENING TO MUSIC
- [ ] MEDITATING
- [ ] JOURNALING
- [ ] READING
- [ ] TALKING TO SOMEONE
- [ ] TIME WITH LOVED ONES
- [ ] TIME WITH A PET
- [ ] GRATITUDE/POSITIVE SELF-TALK
- [ ] TIME OUTSIDE
- [ ] DOWNTIME
- [ ] OTHER: ____________

EVENING REFLECTION

POOR — MY MOOD THIS EVENING — GREAT

1 2 3 4 5 6 7 8 9 10

DIFFICULT EMOTIONS THAT I EXPERIENCED TODAY:

MOMENTS OF HAPPINESS/JOY I EXPERIENCED TODAY:

A SELF-PRAISE OR GRATITUDE:

THIS HELPED ME THE MOST TODAY:

SOMETHING I NEED HELP WITH:

MORNING REFLECTION

DATE ___/___/___

HOURS SLEPT: ______________

POOR		MY MOOD THIS MORNING							GREAT
1	2	3	4	5	6	7	8	9	10

THOUGHTS I WOKE UP WITH / I WOKE UP FEELING:

THE FEELINGS I'M EXPERIENCING MOST RIGHT NOW:

GOALS FOR TODAY:

THINGS THAT CAN WAIT:

HOW I INTEND TO REJUVENATE MY MIND AND BODY TODAY:

- ☐ EXERCISING
- ☐ LISTENING TO MUSIC
- ☐ MEDITATING
- ☐ JOURNALING
- ☐ READING
- ☐ TALKING TO SOMEONE
- ☐ TIME WITH LOVED ONES
- ☐ TIME WITH A PET
- ☐ GRATITUDE/POSITIVE SELF-TALK
- ☐ TIME OUTSIDE
- ☐ DOWNTIME
- ☐ OTHER: ______________

EVENING REFLECTION

POOR MY MOOD THIS EVENING GREAT

1 2 3 4 5 6 7 8 9 10

DIFFICULT EMOTIONS THAT I EXPERIENCED TODAY:

MOMENTS OF HAPPINESS/JOY I EXPERIENCED TODAY:

A SELF-PRAISE OR GRATITUDE:

THIS HELPED ME THE MOST TODAY:

SOMETHING I NEED HELP WITH:

MORNING REFLECTION

DATE ___/___/___

HOURS SLEPT: ____________

MY MOOD THIS MORNING

POOR 1 2 3 4 5 6 7 8 9 10 GREAT

THOUGHTS I WOKE UP WITH / I WOKE UP FEELING:

THE FEELINGS I'M EXPERIENCING MOST RIGHT NOW:

GOALS FOR TODAY:

THINGS THAT CAN WAIT:

HOW I INTEND TO REJUVENATE MY MIND AND BODY TODAY:

- ☐ EXERCISING
- ☐ LISTENING TO MUSIC
- ☐ MEDITATING
- ☐ JOURNALING
- ☐ READING
- ☐ TALKING TO SOMEONE
- ☐ TIME WITH LOVED ONES
- ☐ TIME WITH A PET
- ☐ GRATITUDE/POSITIVE SELF-TALK
- ☐ TIME OUTSIDE
- ☐ DOWNTIME
- ☐ OTHER: ____________

EVENING REFLECTION

POOR MY MOOD THIS EVENING GREAT

1 2 3 4 5 6 7 8 9 10

DIFFICULT EMOTIONS THAT I EXPERIENCED TODAY:

MOMENTS OF HAPPINESS/JOY I EXPERIENCED TODAY:

A SELF-PRAISE OR GRATITUDE:

THIS HELPED ME THE MOST TODAY:

SOMETHING I NEED HELP WITH:

MORNING REFLECTION

DATE ___/___/___

HOURS SLEPT: __________

POOR — MY MOOD THIS MORNING — GREAT

1 2 3 4 5 6 7 8 9 10

THOUGHTS I WOKE UP WITH / I WOKE UP FEELING:

THE FEELINGS I'M EXPERIENCING MOST RIGHT NOW:

GOALS FOR TODAY:

THINGS THAT CAN WAIT:

HOW I INTEND TO REJUVENATE MY MIND AND BODY TODAY:

- [ ] EXERCISING
- [ ] LISTENING TO MUSIC
- [ ] MEDITATING
- [ ] JOURNALING
- [ ] READING
- [ ] TALKING TO SOMEONE
- [ ] TIME WITH LOVED ONES
- [ ] TIME WITH A PET
- [ ] GRATITUDE/POSITIVE SELF-TALK
- [ ] TIME OUTSIDE
- [ ] DOWNTIME
- [ ] OTHER: __________

EVENING REFLECTION

POOR MY MOOD THIS EVENING GREAT

1 2 3 4 5 6 7 8 9 10

DIFFICULT EMOTIONS THAT I EXPERIENCED TODAY:

MOMENTS OF HAPPINESS/JOY I EXPERIENCED TODAY:

A SELF-PRAISE OR GRATITUDE:

THIS HELPED ME THE MOST TODAY:

SOMETHING I NEED HELP WITH:

MORNING REFLECTION

DATE ___/___/___

HOURS SLEPT: __________

MY MOOD THIS MORNING

POOR 1 2 3 4 5 6 7 8 9 10 GREAT

THOUGHTS I WOKE UP WITH / I WOKE UP FEELING:

THE FEELINGS I'M EXPERIENCING MOST RIGHT NOW:

GOALS FOR TODAY:

THINGS THAT CAN WAIT:

HOW I INTEND TO REJUVENATE MY MIND AND BODY TODAY:

- ☐ EXERCISING
- ☐ LISTENING TO MUSIC
- ☐ MEDITATING
- ☐ JOURNALING
- ☐ READING
- ☐ TALKING TO SOMEONE
- ☐ TIME WITH LOVED ONES
- ☐ TIME WITH A PET
- ☐ GRATITUDE/POSITIVE SELF-TALK
- ☐ TIME OUTSIDE
- ☐ DOWNTIME
- ☐ OTHER: __________

EVENING REFLECTION

POOR MY MOOD THIS EVENING GREAT

1 2 3 4 5 6 7 8 9 10

DIFFICULT EMOTIONS THAT I EXPERIENCED TODAY:

MOMENTS OF HAPPINESS/JOY I EXPERIENCED TODAY:

A SELF-PRAISE OR GRATITUDE:

THIS HELPED ME THE MOST TODAY:

SOMETHING I NEED HELP WITH:

MORNING REFLECTION

DATE ___/___/___

HOURS SLEPT: ____________

MY MOOD THIS MORNING

POOR 1 2 3 4 5 6 7 8 9 10 GREAT

THOUGHTS I WOKE UP WITH / I WOKE UP FEELING:

THE FEELINGS I'M EXPERIENCING MOST RIGHT NOW:

GOALS FOR TODAY:

THINGS THAT CAN WAIT:

HOW I INTEND TO REJUVENATE MY MIND AND BODY TODAY:

- ☐ EXERCISING
- ☐ LISTENING TO MUSIC
- ☐ MEDITATING
- ☐ JOURNALING
- ☐ READING
- ☐ TALKING TO SOMEONE
- ☐ TIME WITH LOVED ONES
- ☐ TIME WITH A PET
- ☐ GRATITUDE/POSITIVE SELF-TALK
- ☐ TIME OUTSIDE
- ☐ DOWNTIME
- ☐ OTHER: ____________

EVENING REFLECTION

POOR MY MOOD THIS EVENING GREAT

1 2 3 4 5 6 7 8 9 10

DIFFICULT EMOTIONS THAT I EXPERIENCED TODAY:

MOMENTS OF HAPPINESS/JOY I EXPERIENCED TODAY:

A SELF-PRAISE OR GRATITUDE:

THIS HELPED ME THE MOST TODAY:

SOMETHING I NEED HELP WITH:

MORNING REFLECTION

DATE ___/___/___

HOURS SLEPT: ____________

POOR — MY MOOD THIS MORNING — GREAT

1 2 3 4 5 6 7 8 9 10

THOUGHTS I WOKE UP WITH / I WOKE UP FEELING:

THE FEELINGS I'M EXPERIENCING MOST RIGHT NOW:

GOALS FOR TODAY:

THINGS THAT CAN WAIT:

HOW I INTEND TO REJUVENATE MY MIND AND BODY TODAY:

- ☐ EXERCISING
- ☐ LISTENING TO MUSIC
- ☐ MEDITATING
- ☐ JOURNALING
- ☐ READING
- ☐ TALKING TO SOMEONE
- ☐ TIME WITH LOVED ONES
- ☐ TIME WITH A PET
- ☐ GRATITUDE/POSITIVE SELF-TALK
- ☐ TIME OUTSIDE
- ☐ DOWNTIME
- ☐ OTHER: ____________

EVENING REFLECTION

POOR MY MOOD THIS EVENING GREAT

1 2 3 4 5 6 7 8 9 10

DIFFICULT EMOTIONS THAT I EXPERIENCED TODAY:

MOMENTS OF HAPPINESS/JOY I EXPERIENCED TODAY:

A SELF-PRAISE OR GRATITUDE:

THIS HELPED ME THE MOST TODAY:

SOMETHING I NEED HELP WITH:

MORNING REFLECTION

DATE ___/___/___

HOURS SLEPT: ________

POOR				MY MOOD THIS MORNING					GREAT
1	2	3	4	5	6	7	8	9	10

THOUGHTS I WOKE UP WITH / I WOKE UP FEELING:

THE FEELINGS I'M EXPERIENCING MOST RIGHT NOW:

GOALS FOR TODAY:

THINGS THAT CAN WAIT:

HOW I INTEND TO REJUVENATE MY MIND AND BODY TODAY:

- ☐ EXERCISING
- ☐ LISTENING TO MUSIC
- ☐ MEDITATING
- ☐ JOURNALING
- ☐ READING
- ☐ TALKING TO SOMEONE
- ☐ TIME WITH LOVED ONES
- ☐ TIME WITH A PET
- ☐ GRATITUDE/POSITIVE SELF-TALK
- ☐ TIME OUTSIDE
- ☐ DOWNTIME
- ☐ OTHER: ________

EVENING REFLECTION

POOR — MY MOOD THIS EVENING — GREAT

1 2 3 4 5 6 7 8 9 10

DIFFICULT EMOTIONS THAT I EXPERIENCED TODAY:

MOMENTS OF HAPPINESS/JOY I EXPERIENCED TODAY:

A SELF-PRAISE OR GRATITUDE:

THIS HELPED ME THE MOST TODAY:

SOMETHING I NEED HELP WITH:

MORNING REFLECTION

DATE ___/___/___

HOURS SLEPT: ____________

MY MOOD THIS MORNING

POOR 1 2 3 4 5 6 7 8 9 10 GREAT

THOUGHTS I WOKE UP WITH / I WOKE UP FEELING:

THE FEELINGS I'M EXPERIENCING MOST RIGHT NOW:

GOALS FOR TODAY:

THINGS THAT CAN WAIT:

HOW I INTEND TO REJUVENATE MY MIND AND BODY TODAY:

- ☐ EXERCISING
- ☐ LISTENING TO MUSIC
- ☐ MEDITATING
- ☐ JOURNALING
- ☐ READING
- ☐ TALKING TO SOMEONE
- ☐ TIME WITH LOVED ONES
- ☐ TIME WITH A PET
- ☐ GRATITUDE/POSITIVE SELF-TALK
- ☐ TIME OUTSIDE
- ☐ DOWNTIME
- ☐ OTHER: ____________

EVENING REFLECTION

POOR — MY MOOD THIS EVENING — GREAT

1 2 3 4 5 6 7 8 9 10

DIFFICULT EMOTIONS THAT I EXPERIENCED TODAY:

MOMENTS OF HAPPINESS/JOY I EXPERIENCED TODAY:

A SELF-PRAISE OR GRATITUDE:

THIS HELPED ME THE MOST TODAY:

SOMETHING I NEED HELP WITH:

MORNING REFLECTION

DATE ___/___/___

HOURS SLEPT: ________

MY MOOD THIS MORNING

POOR 1 2 3 4 5 6 7 8 9 10 GREAT

THOUGHTS I WOKE UP WITH / I WOKE UP FEELING:

THE FEELINGS I'M EXPERIENCING MOST RIGHT NOW:

GOALS FOR TODAY:

THINGS THAT CAN WAIT:

HOW I INTEND TO REJUVENATE MY MIND AND BODY TODAY:

- ☐ EXERCISING
- ☐ LISTENING TO MUSIC
- ☐ MEDITATING
- ☐ JOURNALING
- ☐ READING
- ☐ TALKING TO SOMEONE
- ☐ TIME WITH LOVED ONES
- ☐ TIME WITH A PET
- ☐ GRATITUDE/POSITIVE SELF-TALK
- ☐ TIME OUTSIDE
- ☐ DOWNTIME
- ☐ OTHER: ________

EVENING REFLECTION

POOR MY MOOD THIS EVENING GREAT

1 2 3 4 5 6 7 8 9 10

DIFFICULT EMOTIONS THAT I EXPERIENCED TODAY:

MOMENTS OF HAPPINESS/JOY I EXPERIENCED TODAY:

A SELF-PRAISE OR GRATITUDE:

THIS HELPED ME THE MOST TODAY:

SOMETHING I NEED HELP WITH:

MORNING REFLECTION

DATE ___/___/___

HOURS SLEPT: ____________

MY MOOD THIS MORNING

POOR 1 2 3 4 5 6 7 8 9 10 GREAT

THOUGHTS I WOKE UP WITH / I WOKE UP FEELING:

THE FEELINGS I'M EXPERIENCING MOST RIGHT NOW:

GOALS FOR TODAY:

THINGS THAT CAN WAIT:

HOW I INTEND TO REJUVENATE MY MIND AND BODY TODAY:

- ☐ EXERCISING
- ☐ LISTENING TO MUSIC
- ☐ MEDITATING
- ☐ JOURNALING
- ☐ READING
- ☐ TALKING TO SOMEONE
- ☐ TIME WITH LOVED ONES
- ☐ TIME WITH A PET
- ☐ GRATITUDE/POSITIVE SELF-TALK
- ☐ TIME OUTSIDE
- ☐ DOWNTIME
- ☐ OTHER: ____________

EVENING REFLECTION

POOR — MY MOOD THIS EVENING — GREAT

1 2 3 4 5 6 7 8 9 10

DIFFICULT EMOTIONS THAT I EXPERIENCED TODAY:

MOMENTS OF HAPPINESS/JOY I EXPERIENCED TODAY:

A SELF-PRAISE OR GRATITUDE:

THIS HELPED ME THE MOST TODAY:

SOMETHING I NEED HELP WITH:

MORNING REFLECTION

DATE ___/___/___

HOURS SLEPT: ______

MY MOOD THIS MORNING

POOR 1 2 3 4 5 6 7 8 9 10 GREAT

THOUGHTS I WOKE UP WITH / I WOKE UP FEELING:

THE FEELINGS I'M EXPERIENCING MOST RIGHT NOW:

GOALS FOR TODAY:

THINGS THAT CAN WAIT:

HOW I INTEND TO REJUVENATE MY MIND AND BODY TODAY:

- ☐ EXERCISING
- ☐ LISTENING TO MUSIC
- ☐ MEDITATING
- ☐ JOURNALING
- ☐ READING
- ☐ TALKING TO SOMEONE
- ☐ TIME WITH LOVED ONES
- ☐ TIME WITH A PET
- ☐ GRATITUDE/POSITIVE SELF-TALK
- ☐ TIME OUTSIDE
- ☐ DOWNTIME
- ☐ OTHER: ______

EVENING REFLECTION

POOR MY MOOD THIS EVENING GREAT

1 2 3 4 5 6 7 8 9 10

DIFFICULT EMOTIONS THAT I EXPERIENCED TODAY:

MOMENTS OF HAPPINESS/JOY I EXPERIENCED TODAY:

A SELF-PRAISE OR GRATITUDE:

THIS HELPED ME THE MOST TODAY:

SOMETHING I NEED HELP WITH:

MORNING REFLECTION

DATE ___/___/___

HOURS SLEPT: ______

POOR — MY MOOD THIS MORNING — GREAT

1 2 3 4 5 6 7 8 9 10

THOUGHTS I WOKE UP WITH / I WOKE UP FEELING:

THE FEELINGS I'M EXPERIENCING MOST RIGHT NOW:

GOALS FOR TODAY:

THINGS THAT CAN WAIT:

HOW I INTEND TO REJUVENATE MY MIND AND BODY TODAY:

- ☐ EXERCISING
- ☐ LISTENING TO MUSIC
- ☐ MEDITATING
- ☐ JOURNALING
- ☐ READING
- ☐ TALKING TO SOMEONE
- ☐ TIME WITH LOVED ONES
- ☐ TIME WITH A PET
- ☐ GRATITUDE/POSITIVE SELF-TALK
- ☐ TIME OUTSIDE
- ☐ DOWNTIME
- ☐ OTHER: ______

EVENING REFLECTION

POOR MY MOOD THIS EVENING GREAT

1 2 3 4 5 6 7 8 9 10

DIFFICULT EMOTIONS THAT I EXPERIENCED TODAY:

MOMENTS OF HAPPINESS/JOY I EXPERIENCED TODAY:

A SELF-PRAISE OR GRATITUDE:

THIS HELPED ME THE MOST TODAY:

SOMETHING I NEED HELP WITH:

MORNING REFLECTION

DATE ___/___/___

HOURS SLEPT: ______

MY MOOD THIS MORNING

POOR 1 2 3 4 5 6 7 8 9 10 GREAT

THOUGHTS I WOKE UP WITH / I WOKE UP FEELING:

THE FEELINGS I'M EXPERIENCING MOST RIGHT NOW:

GOALS FOR TODAY:

THINGS THAT CAN WAIT:

HOW I INTEND TO REJUVENATE MY MIND AND BODY TODAY:

- ☐ EXERCISING
- ☐ LISTENING TO MUSIC
- ☐ MEDITATING
- ☐ JOURNALING
- ☐ READING
- ☐ TALKING TO SOMEONE
- ☐ TIME WITH LOVED ONES
- ☐ TIME WITH A PET
- ☐ GRATITUDE/POSITIVE SELF-TALK
- ☐ TIME OUTSIDE
- ☐ DOWNTIME
- ☐ OTHER: ______

EVENING REFLECTION

POOR MY MOOD THIS EVENING GREAT

1 2 3 4 5 6 7 8 9 10

DIFFICULT EMOTIONS THAT I EXPERIENCED TODAY:

MOMENTS OF HAPPINESS/JOY I EXPERIENCED TODAY:

A SELF-PRAISE OR GRATITUDE:

THIS HELPED ME THE MOST TODAY:

SOMETHING I NEED HELP WITH:

MORNING REFLECTION

DATE ___/___/___

HOURS SLEPT: ____________

POOR — MY MOOD THIS MORNING — GREAT

1 2 3 4 5 6 7 8 9 10

THOUGHTS I WOKE UP WITH / I WOKE UP FEELING:

THE FEELINGS I'M EXPERIENCING MOST RIGHT NOW:

GOALS FOR TODAY:

THINGS THAT CAN WAIT:

HOW I INTEND TO REJUVENATE MY MIND AND BODY TODAY:

- ☐ EXERCISING
- ☐ LISTENING TO MUSIC
- ☐ MEDITATING
- ☐ JOURNALING
- ☐ READING
- ☐ TALKING TO SOMEONE
- ☐ TIME WITH LOVED ONES
- ☐ TIME WITH A PET
- ☐ GRATITUDE/POSITIVE SELF-TALK
- ☐ TIME OUTSIDE
- ☐ DOWNTIME
- ☐ OTHER: ____________

EVENING REFLECTION

POOR MY MOOD THIS EVENING GREAT

1 2 3 4 5 6 7 8 9 10

DIFFICULT EMOTIONS THAT I EXPERIENCED TODAY:

MOMENTS OF HAPPINESS/JOY I EXPERIENCED TODAY:

A SELF-PRAISE OR GRATITUDE:

THIS HELPED ME THE MOST TODAY:

SOMETHING I NEED HELP WITH:

MORNING REFLECTION

DATE ___/___/___

HOURS SLEPT:	POOR			MY MOOD THIS MORNING						GREAT
________	1	2	3	4	5	6	7	8	9	10

THOUGHTS I WOKE UP WITH / I WOKE UP FEELING:

THE FEELINGS I'M EXPERIENCING MOST RIGHT NOW:

GOALS FOR TODAY:

THINGS THAT CAN WAIT:

HOW I INTEND TO REJUVENATE MY MIND AND BODY TODAY:

- ☐ EXERCISING
- ☐ LISTENING TO MUSIC
- ☐ MEDITATING
- ☐ JOURNALING
- ☐ READING
- ☐ TALKING TO SOMEONE
- ☐ TIME WITH LOVED ONES
- ☐ TIME WITH A PET
- ☐ GRATITUDE/POSITIVE SELF-TALK
- ☐ TIME OUTSIDE
- ☐ DOWNTIME
- ☐ OTHER: ________

EVENING REFLECTION

POOR MY MOOD THIS EVENING GREAT

1 2 3 4 5 6 7 8 9 10

DIFFICULT EMOTIONS THAT I EXPERIENCED TODAY:

MOMENTS OF HAPPINESS/JOY I EXPERIENCED TODAY:

A SELF-PRAISE OR GRATITUDE:

THIS HELPED ME THE MOST TODAY:

SOMETHING I NEED HELP WITH:

MORNING REFLECTION

DATE ___/___/___

HOURS SLEPT: ________

POOR — MY MOOD THIS MORNING — GREAT

1 2 3 4 5 6 7 8 9 10

THOUGHTS I WOKE UP WITH / I WOKE UP FEELING:

THE FEELINGS I'M EXPERIENCING MOST RIGHT NOW:

GOALS FOR TODAY:

THINGS THAT CAN WAIT:

HOW I INTEND TO REJUVENATE MY MIND AND BODY TODAY:

- ☐ EXERCISING
- ☐ LISTENING TO MUSIC
- ☐ MEDITATING
- ☐ JOURNALING
- ☐ READING
- ☐ TALKING TO SOMEONE
- ☐ TIME WITH LOVED ONES
- ☐ TIME WITH A PET
- ☐ GRATITUDE/POSITIVE SELF-TALK
- ☐ TIME OUTSIDE
- ☐ DOWNTIME
- ☐ OTHER: ________

EVENING REFLECTION

POOR MY MOOD THIS EVENING GREAT

1 2 3 4 5 6 7 8 9 10

DIFFICULT EMOTIONS THAT I EXPERIENCED TODAY:

MOMENTS OF HAPPINESS/JOY I EXPERIENCED TODAY:

A SELF-PRAISE OR GRATITUDE:

THIS HELPED ME THE MOST TODAY:

SOMETHING I NEED HELP WITH:

MORNING REFLECTION

DATE ___/___/___

HOURS SLEPT: ______

MY MOOD THIS MORNING

POOR 1 2 3 4 5 6 7 8 9 10 GREAT

THOUGHTS I WOKE UP WITH / I WOKE UP FEELING:

THE FEELINGS I'M EXPERIENCING MOST RIGHT NOW:

GOALS FOR TODAY:

THINGS THAT CAN WAIT:

HOW I INTEND TO REJUVENATE MY MIND AND BODY TODAY:

- ☐ EXERCISING
- ☐ LISTENING TO MUSIC
- ☐ MEDITATING
- ☐ JOURNALING
- ☐ READING
- ☐ TALKING TO SOMEONE
- ☐ TIME WITH LOVED ONES
- ☐ TIME WITH A PET
- ☐ GRATITUDE/POSITIVE SELF-TALK
- ☐ TIME OUTSIDE
- ☐ DOWNTIME
- ☐ OTHER: ______

EVENING REFLECTION

POOR — MY MOOD THIS EVENING — GREAT

1 2 3 4 5 6 7 8 9 10

DIFFICULT EMOTIONS THAT I EXPERIENCED TODAY:

MOMENTS OF HAPPINESS/JOY I EXPERIENCED TODAY:

A SELF-PRAISE OR GRATITUDE:

THIS HELPED ME THE MOST TODAY:

SOMETHING I NEED HELP WITH:

MORNING REFLECTION

DATE ___/___/___

HOURS SLEPT: ____________

MY MOOD THIS MORNING

POOR									GREAT
1	2	3	4	5	6	7	8	9	10

THOUGHTS I WOKE UP WITH / I WOKE UP FEELING:

THE FEELINGS I'M EXPERIENCING MOST RIGHT NOW:

GOALS FOR TODAY:

THINGS THAT CAN WAIT:

HOW I INTEND TO REJUVENATE MY MIND AND BODY TODAY:

- ☐ EXERCISING
- ☐ LISTENING TO MUSIC
- ☐ MEDITATING
- ☐ JOURNALING
- ☐ READING
- ☐ TALKING TO SOMEONE
- ☐ TIME WITH LOVED ONES
- ☐ TIME WITH A PET
- ☐ GRATITUDE/POSITIVE SELF-TALK
- ☐ TIME OUTSIDE
- ☐ DOWNTIME
- ☐ OTHER: ____________

EVENING REFLECTION

POOR MY MOOD THIS EVENING GREAT

1 2 3 4 5 6 7 8 9 10

DIFFICULT EMOTIONS THAT I EXPERIENCED TODAY:

MOMENTS OF HAPPINESS/JOY I EXPERIENCED TODAY:

A SELF-PRAISE OR GRATITUDE:

THIS HELPED ME THE MOST TODAY:

SOMETHING I NEED HELP WITH:

MORNING REFLECTION

DATE ___/___/___

HOURS SLEPT: ____________

MY MOOD THIS MORNING

POOR 1 2 3 4 5 6 7 8 9 10 GREAT

THOUGHTS I WOKE UP WITH / I WOKE UP FEELING:

THE FEELINGS I'M EXPERIENCING MOST RIGHT NOW:

GOALS FOR TODAY:

THINGS THAT CAN WAIT:

HOW I INTEND TO REJUVENATE MY MIND AND BODY TODAY:

- [ ] EXERCISING
- [ ] LISTENING TO MUSIC
- [ ] MEDITATING
- [ ] JOURNALING
- [ ] READING
- [ ] TALKING TO SOMEONE
- [ ] TIME WITH LOVED ONES
- [ ] TIME WITH A PET
- [ ] GRATITUDE/POSITIVE SELF-TALK
- [ ] TIME OUTSIDE
- [ ] DOWNTIME
- [ ] OTHER: ____________

EVENING REFLECTION

POOR | MY MOOD THIS EVENING | GREAT

1 2 3 4 5 6 7 8 9 10

DIFFICULT EMOTIONS THAT I EXPERIENCED TODAY:

MOMENTS OF HAPPINESS/JOY I EXPERIENCED TODAY:

A SELF-PRAISE OR GRATITUDE:

THIS HELPED ME THE MOST TODAY:

SOMETHING I NEED HELP WITH:

MORNING REFLECTION

DATE ___/___/___

HOURS SLEPT: ____________

POOR		MY MOOD THIS MORNING							GREAT
1	2	3	4	5	6	7	8	9	10

THOUGHTS I WOKE UP WITH / I WOKE UP FEELING:

THE FEELINGS I'M EXPERIENCING MOST RIGHT NOW:

GOALS FOR TODAY:

THINGS THAT CAN WAIT:

HOW I INTEND TO REJUVENATE MY MIND AND BODY TODAY:

- ☐ EXERCISING
- ☐ LISTENING TO MUSIC
- ☐ MEDITATING
- ☐ JOURNALING
- ☐ READING
- ☐ TALKING TO SOMEONE
- ☐ TIME WITH LOVED ONES
- ☐ TIME WITH A PET
- ☐ GRATITUDE/POSITIVE SELF-TALK
- ☐ TIME OUTSIDE
- ☐ DOWNTIME
- ☐ OTHER: ____________

EVENING REFLECTION

POOR MY MOOD THIS EVENING GREAT

1 2 3 4 5 6 7 8 9 10

DIFFICULT EMOTIONS THAT I EXPERIENCED TODAY:

MOMENTS OF HAPPINESS/JOY I EXPERIENCED TODAY:

A SELF-PRAISE OR GRATITUDE:

THIS HELPED ME THE MOST TODAY:

SOMETHING I NEED HELP WITH:

MORNING REFLECTION

DATE ___/___/___

HOURS SLEPT: ______

POOR — MY MOOD THIS MORNING — GREAT

1 2 3 4 5 6 7 8 9 10

THOUGHTS I WOKE UP WITH / I WOKE UP FEELING:

THE FEELINGS I'M EXPERIENCING MOST RIGHT NOW:

GOALS FOR TODAY:

THINGS THAT CAN WAIT:

HOW I INTEND TO REJUVENATE MY MIND AND BODY TODAY:

- ☐ EXERCISING
- ☐ LISTENING TO MUSIC
- ☐ MEDITATING
- ☐ JOURNALING
- ☐ READING
- ☐ TALKING TO SOMEONE
- ☐ TIME WITH LOVED ONES
- ☐ TIME WITH A PET
- ☐ GRATITUDE/POSITIVE SELF-TALK
- ☐ TIME OUTSIDE
- ☐ DOWNTIME
- ☐ OTHER: ______

EVENING REFLECTION

POOR MY MOOD THIS EVENING GREAT

1 2 3 4 5 6 7 8 9 10

DIFFICULT EMOTIONS THAT I EXPERIENCED TODAY:

MOMENTS OF HAPPINESS/JOY I EXPERIENCED TODAY:

A SELF-PRAISE OR GRATITUDE:

THIS HELPED ME THE MOST TODAY:

SOMETHING I NEED HELP WITH:

MORNING REFLECTION

DATE ___/___/___

HOURS SLEPT: ____________

POOR	MY MOOD THIS MORNING								GREAT
1	2	3	4	5	6	7	8	9	10

THOUGHTS I WOKE UP WITH / I WOKE UP FEELING:

THE FEELINGS I'M EXPERIENCING MOST RIGHT NOW:

GOALS FOR TODAY:

THINGS THAT CAN WAIT:

HOW I INTEND TO REJUVENATE MY MIND AND BODY TODAY:

- ☐ EXERCISING
- ☐ LISTENING TO MUSIC
- ☐ MEDITATING
- ☐ JOURNALING
- ☐ READING
- ☐ TALKING TO SOMEONE
- ☐ TIME WITH LOVED ONES
- ☐ TIME WITH A PET
- ☐ GRATITUDE/POSITIVE SELF-TALK
- ☐ TIME OUTSIDE
- ☐ DOWNTIME
- ☐ OTHER: ____________

EVENING REFLECTION

POOR MY MOOD THIS EVENING GREAT

1 2 3 4 5 6 7 8 9 10

DIFFICULT EMOTIONS THAT I EXPERIENCED TODAY:

MOMENTS OF HAPPINESS/JOY I EXPERIENCED TODAY:

A SELF-PRAISE OR GRATITUDE:

THIS HELPED ME THE MOST TODAY:

SOMETHING I NEED HELP WITH:

MORNING REFLECTION

DATE ___/___/___

HOURS SLEPT: ________

MY MOOD THIS MORNING

POOR 1 2 3 4 5 6 7 8 9 10 GREAT

THOUGHTS I WOKE UP WITH / I WOKE UP FEELING:

THE FEELINGS I'M EXPERIENCING MOST RIGHT NOW:

GOALS FOR TODAY:

THINGS THAT CAN WAIT:

HOW I INTEND TO REJUVENATE MY MIND AND BODY TODAY:

- ☐ EXERCISING
- ☐ LISTENING TO MUSIC
- ☐ MEDITATING
- ☐ JOURNALING
- ☐ READING
- ☐ TALKING TO SOMEONE
- ☐ TIME WITH LOVED ONES
- ☐ TIME WITH A PET
- ☐ GRATITUDE/POSITIVE SELF-TALK
- ☐ TIME OUTSIDE
- ☐ DOWNTIME
- ☐ OTHER: ________

EVENING REFLECTION

POOR MY MOOD THIS EVENING GREAT

1 2 3 4 5 6 7 8 9 10

DIFFICULT EMOTIONS THAT I EXPERIENCED TODAY:

MOMENTS OF HAPPINESS/JOY I EXPERIENCED TODAY:

A SELF-PRAISE OR GRATITUDE:

THIS HELPED ME THE MOST TODAY:

SOMETHING I NEED HELP WITH:

MORNING REFLECTION

DATE ___/___/___

HOURS SLEPT: ____________

POOR			MY MOOD THIS MORNING						GREAT
1	2	3	4	5	6	7	8	9	10

THOUGHTS I WOKE UP WITH / I WOKE UP FEELING:

THE FEELINGS I'M EXPERIENCING MOST RIGHT NOW:

GOALS FOR TODAY:

THINGS THAT CAN WAIT:

HOW I INTEND TO REJUVENATE MY MIND AND BODY TODAY:

- ☐ EXERCISING
- ☐ LISTENING TO MUSIC
- ☐ MEDITATING
- ☐ JOURNALING
- ☐ READING
- ☐ TALKING TO SOMEONE
- ☐ TIME WITH LOVED ONES
- ☐ TIME WITH A PET
- ☐ GRATITUDE/POSITIVE SELF-TALK
- ☐ TIME OUTSIDE
- ☐ DOWNTIME
- ☐ OTHER: ____________

EVENING REFLECTION

POOR | MY MOOD THIS EVENING | GREAT

1 2 3 4 5 6 7 8 9 10

DIFFICULT EMOTIONS THAT I EXPERIENCED TODAY:

MOMENTS OF HAPPINESS/JOY I EXPERIENCED TODAY:

A SELF-PRAISE OR GRATITUDE:

THIS HELPED ME THE MOST TODAY:

SOMETHING I NEED HELP WITH:

MORNING REFLECTION

DATE ___/___/___

HOURS SLEPT: ________

MY MOOD THIS MORNING

POOR 1 2 3 4 5 6 7 8 9 10 GREAT

THOUGHTS I WOKE UP WITH / I WOKE UP FEELING:

THE FEELINGS I'M EXPERIENCING MOST RIGHT NOW:

GOALS FOR TODAY:

THINGS THAT CAN WAIT:

HOW I INTEND TO REJUVENATE MY MIND AND BODY TODAY:

- [ ] EXERCISING
- [ ] LISTENING TO MUSIC
- [ ] MEDITATING
- [ ] JOURNALING
- [ ] READING
- [ ] TALKING TO SOMEONE
- [ ] TIME WITH LOVED ONES
- [ ] TIME WITH A PET
- [ ] GRATITUDE/POSITIVE SELF-TALK
- [ ] TIME OUTSIDE
- [ ] DOWNTIME
- [ ] OTHER: ________

EVENING REFLECTION

POOR MY MOOD THIS EVENING GREAT

1 2 3 4 5 6 7 8 9 10

DIFFICULT EMOTIONS THAT I EXPERIENCED TODAY:

MOMENTS OF HAPPINESS/JOY I EXPERIENCED TODAY:

A SELF-PRAISE OR GRATITUDE:

THIS HELPED ME THE MOST TODAY:

SOMETHING I NEED HELP WITH:

MORNING REFLECTION

DATE ___/___/___

HOURS SLEPT: ___________

MY MOOD THIS MORNING

POOR 1 2 3 4 5 6 7 8 9 10 GREAT

THOUGHTS I WOKE UP WITH / I WOKE UP FEELING:

THE FEELINGS I'M EXPERIENCING MOST RIGHT NOW:

GOALS FOR TODAY:

THINGS THAT CAN WAIT:

HOW I INTEND TO REJUVENATE MY MIND AND BODY TODAY:

- ☐ EXERCISING
- ☐ LISTENING TO MUSIC
- ☐ MEDITATING
- ☐ JOURNALING
- ☐ READING
- ☐ TALKING TO SOMEONE
- ☐ TIME WITH LOVED ONES
- ☐ TIME WITH A PET
- ☐ GRATITUDE/POSITIVE SELF-TALK
- ☐ TIME OUTSIDE
- ☐ DOWNTIME
- ☐ OTHER: ___________

EVENING REFLECTION

POOR MY MOOD THIS EVENING GREAT

1 2 3 4 5 6 7 8 9 10

DIFFICULT EMOTIONS THAT I EXPERIENCED TODAY:

MOMENTS OF HAPPINESS/JOY I EXPERIENCED TODAY:

A SELF-PRAISE OR GRATITUDE:

THIS HELPED ME THE MOST TODAY:

SOMETHING I NEED HELP WITH:

MORNING REFLECTION

DATE ___/___/___

HOURS SLEPT: ____________

MY MOOD THIS MORNING

POOR 1 2 3 4 5 6 7 8 9 10 GREAT

THOUGHTS I WOKE UP WITH / I WOKE UP FEELING:

THE FEELINGS I'M EXPERIENCING MOST RIGHT NOW:

GOALS FOR TODAY:

THINGS THAT CAN WAIT:

HOW I INTEND TO REJUVENATE MY MIND AND BODY TODAY:

- ☐ EXERCISING
- ☐ LISTENING TO MUSIC
- ☐ MEDITATING
- ☐ JOURNALING
- ☐ READING
- ☐ TALKING TO SOMEONE
- ☐ TIME WITH LOVED ONES
- ☐ TIME WITH A PET
- ☐ GRATITUDE/POSITIVE SELF-TALK
- ☐ TIME OUTSIDE
- ☐ DOWNTIME
- ☐ OTHER: ____________

EVENING REFLECTION

POOR MY MOOD THIS EVENING GREAT

1 2 3 4 5 6 7 8 9 10

DIFFICULT EMOTIONS THAT I EXPERIENCED TODAY:

MOMENTS OF HAPPINESS/JOY I EXPERIENCED TODAY:

A SELF-PRAISE OR GRATITUDE:

THIS HELPED ME THE MOST TODAY:

SOMETHING I NEED HELP WITH:

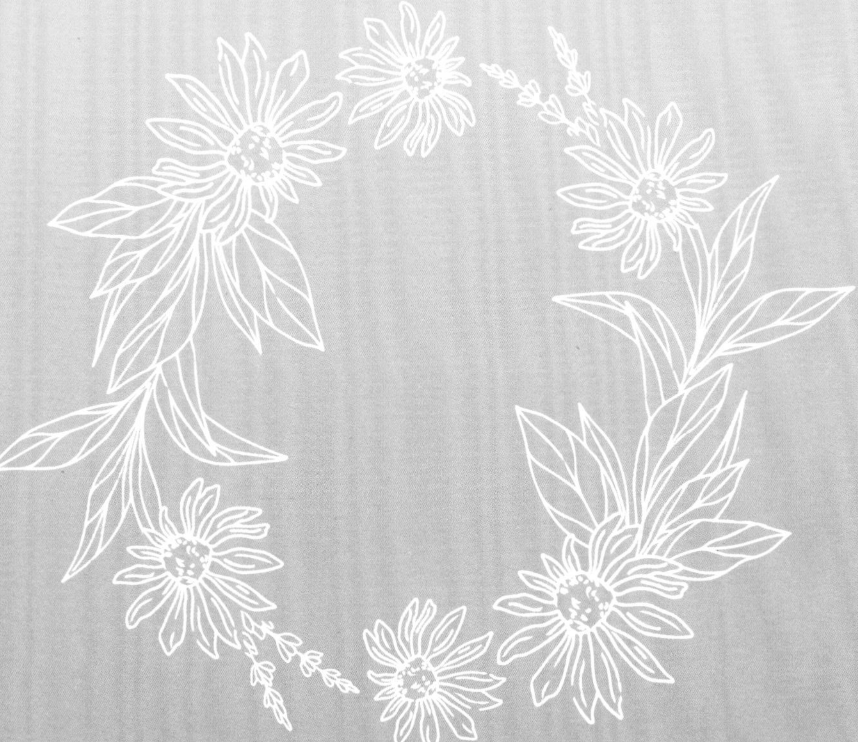

INSIGHTS

A Mandala Journal

www.mandalaearth.com

Art direction and design by Ashley Quackenbush

MANUFACTURED IN CHINA

10 9 8 7 6 5 4 3 2 1